T0267079

Harmony *in* *Impact*

Navigating Tensions in Social Entrepreneurship

DR. USHA CHAUDHARY

ISBN: 979-8-35094-843-1

DEDICATIONS

To my parents for their guidance, perseverance, and sacrifices; my husband for his ongoing support; and my amazing children for their boundless love, warmth, and encouragement – I hope this inspires you to continue your lifelong journey of learning, service, and growth, as you have inspired me to become a better version of myself.

(EPIGRAPH)

*The best way to find yourself is to lose yourself
in the service of others.*

—Mahatma Gandhi

CONTENTS

LIST OF FIGURES

PREFACE

My interest in the social sector and drive for social impact have been fueled by several factors, some of which were instilled very early in life. Having spent a part of my childhood and adolescence in rural India and Nepal, I had witnessed and was moved by the poverty and living conditions of underserved individuals and families in several communities. I recall being overcome with sadness on seeing children my age and younger begging in the streets, wondering what led to their financial hardship, how they lived and survived from one day to the next, whether they had access to school education, and what could be done to improve their living conditions. A few decades later, during my MBA program residency, I had the opportunity to work on a project in Ghana and was deeply struck by the impoverished living conditions in some regions of the country. I remember visiting cocoa farms and a fishing village and speaking with farmers and fishermen who struggled to make a living to support their families.

My vast professional experience as an executive and board member of several global non-profit organizations have also greatly sensitized me to the social, humanitarian, and environmental challenges that exist around the world. I was blessed to have grown up in a household that valued ongoing learning and service to others, parents who exemplified these core values through their daily deeds and actions, and several family members who have spent most of their lives in social services in areas including childhood education, women empowerment, healthcare accessibility, and economic sustainability. It is no wonder that I have a deep passion for social impact and have pursued it throughout my life.

Seeing the commonalities related to the challenges of launching and operating a social enterprise, my personal and professional journey has been centered on making an impact on and helping society through my work. I am hoping that my book will help and motivate current and future social entrepreneurs to continue to make an impact in the world by helping to solve societal problems to enable a safer and better world for our future generations.

One might ask, "What societal problems am I referring to?" Well, many notable scientists and scholars have asserted that humanity is on the path to extinction and have gone so far as to predict that the people who are alive today may be one of the last generations of the human species on Earth. Whether this extinction occurs due to natural causes or is self-inflicted by humans, it is an undeniable fact that societal challenges in areas such as climate change, healthcare, and the global pandemic, poverty and hunger, social justice and equality, crime and violence, human rights and trafficking, and financial and political corruption, to name a few, are continuing to escalate and multiply on a global scale.

Unfortunately, the public and private sectors have not addressed these problems adequately, making the need for social entrepreneurs and social enterprises essential. Further, according to the World Economic Forum, nearly 40 percent of social enterprises fail within one year, approximately 45 percent of new social enterprises survive past three years, and less than 10 percent survive past six years, due primarily to the lack of financial resources, advocacy, and governance. Therefore, we need to support social entrepreneurs and social enterprises to solve these and other social issues at the local, national, and global levels.

It is no surprise that in fulfillment of my recent doctoral program, I chose to research social entrepreneurship to gain greater insights into the many challenges that are faced by social entrepreneurs during the launch and operating phases of their social enterprise and how they manage, mitigate, or overcome such challenges. My qualitative research was based on the grounded theory research method (Charmaz, 2006) to seek insights into the balancing act that social entrepreneurs must engage in to cope with and manage various conflicts, tensions, and trade-offs in launching and operating a social enterprise. The grounded theory method is a systematic and flexible method for collecting, coding, and analyzing qualitative data to develop emergent theories from the underlying data. This is an inductive approach to reviewing data, coding, and synthesizing data, and analyzing the patterns that emerge, that led to the development of relevant theories.

My rationale for using the qualitative grounded theory research method, instead of the quantitative method, was threefold. First, the nature of my research required deep probing into the social entrepreneurs' thoughts, beliefs, motivations, and intentions that could best be accomplished through one-on-one, face-to-face or virtual interviews. Second, there is no existing quantitative data available that could be utilized for this research. Finally, using surveys to gather quantitative data and quantitative methods to show causality and relationships would be insufficient in reaching an adequate understanding of the issues or drawing meaningful conclusions.

Therefore, my primary data source included interviews with 22 renowned social entrepreneurs from a variety of social enterprises. I selected social entrepreneurs in social enterprises of varying sizes, mission focus areas, organizational life cycles, and geographies. Specifically, of the 22 social entrepreneurs, 14 were male and 8 were female; 9 were US-centric, 5 were non-US-centric, 8 operated globally; 16 were founders and co-founders, whereas 6 were non-founding executives or managers. This mix ensured the credibility and diversity of experiences and thoughts in my data set.

In this book, I will share the results of my research by outlining the competing, contradictory, and conflicting challenges and tensions that social entrepreneurs face in launching and operating a social enterprise; how they manage and balance these challenges; and the various coping mechanisms they must deploy to both respond to and survive in facing these inherent tensions. I will also provide a typology of the unique characteristics and attributes that successful social entrepreneurs possess that enable them to survive and thrive in challenging environments. Throughout the book, I will refer to the experiences of many of these social entrepreneurs as exemplars, both to highlight and emphasize my findings.

My hope is that this book will help current and future social entrepreneurs to better understand the many challenges and trade-offs involved in launching and operating a social enterprise provide solutions for how to manage and balance these trade-offs. In doing so, social entrepreneurs may be able to avoid certain pitfalls, thereby improving their likelihood of success so that they can help shape a better future for our society and world.

ACKNOWLEDGEMENTS

This book would not have been possible without the love and support of my husband, Vinod, and my amazing children, Masoom and Nabeel. They have always been a source of endless encouragement and always available to help whenever I have needed it. I also want to acknowledge my deceased parents, Kanhaiya Lal Rai and Shanti Devi, for the values they instilled in me, values centered on service, sacrifice, and resilience. I greatly appreciate my siblings and their spouses – Dhananjaya and India Kumar, Manorama and Arthur Lovelace, and Siddhanta and Lina Vikram – for their love, support, and ongoing service to their communities at home and overseas, covering a range of areas including education, healthcare, women and children empowerment, and economic sustainability. I am blessed to be in a family that values selfless giving and encourages ongoing knowledge, self-learning, and growth.

I am forever grateful to the social entrepreneurs who agreed to be interviewed for my research and form the basis for much of the content of this book. I continue to be inspired by each of them. Several interviewees opted to remain anonymous; however, those who agreed to be named include Scott Beale, Nicolas Cuttriss, Tom Dillon, Bill Drayton, Robert Egger, Dhananjaya Kumar, Indira Kumar, Rajiv Malhotra, Roshan Paul, Scott Rechler, Carrie Rich, Tessie San Martin, Burck Smith, Nancy Welsh, and Gretchen Zucker.

Last but certainly not least, my research would not have been possible without Danny Tzabbar and Rajiv Nag, who served as Co-Chairs for my doctoral dissertation at Drexel University. They were the beacons throughout my incredible journey into the depths of examining the social entrepreneurship domain. Their teaching and guidance expanded my critical thinking and further fueled my love for knowledge and learning.

INTRODUCTION

Developing and underdeveloped economies make up more than 80 percent of the world's population. Most people living in these economies are at the bottom of the socio-economic pyramid (Esposito, 2012), often called the Base of the Pyramid (BoP). Of the nearly five billion people in this category, approximately 60 percent of the population are poor by any measure, live and function in an informal market ecosystem, and earn less than $8 per person per day. The BoP segment faces persistent poverty and a huge demand-supply gap in the formal market ecosystem for the fulfillment of its basic needs.

Unfortunately, the initiatives undertaken by the traditional institutional constructs like government agencies, non-government organizations (NGOs), non-profit organizations, and socially motivated corporate entities have achieved limited success in bridging the socio-economic gap or in generating the desired level of social impact, scalability, and reach for the BoP. These limitations have led to the evolution of social entrepreneurship as an emerging market-based alternative for having a scalable socio-economic impact on the BoP. Social entrepreneurship involves a social entrepreneur as a change agent and a social enterprise as an organizational entity that considers the BoP segment as its primary stakeholder or customer. These enterprises are driven by the philosophy of "Serve and Survive at the BoP."

To emphasize a point made earlier, we are faced with numerous threats and systemic challenges of global proportions today, including the degradation of the quality and accessibility of our education system; escalating race and gender inequality; worsening poverty; a serious public health crisis; the deterioration of the supply of clean water; climate change and other threats to our environmental sustainability; numerous human rights issues; and the potentially negative societal impacts of the technology revolution, including generative AI, if left uncontrolled, unmanaged, and unregulated. In addition to the global economic, social, and material progress required, the individual transition from knowledge to wisdom, attained from greater focus on self-inquiry and intellectual growth, connecton with nature, living a healthy lifestyle, and advancing collective welfare, is essential for human and societal evolution. Governments and corporations have largely ignored many of these challenges. Therefore, enterprises have emerged to provide scalable and replicable solutions to help address the world's biggest challenges. This development signals the need for more and perhaps a different breed of social entrepreneurs and enterprises to tackle these global and systemic issues.

Having experienced and observed some of these challenges firsthand, social entrepreneurs undoubtedly face numerous challenges in launching and operating a social enterprise. Meeting these challenges requires a great deal of agility, creativity, resilience, and tenacity in managing and mitigating the obstacles and addressing the various tensions and trade-offs that result from it. Oftentimes, these challenges can become insurmountable, or the social entrepreneur may simply not be equipped to deal with them, resulting in the failure of the social entrepreneur and/or the social enterprise. Before we begin to explore these topics further, it is important to first understand the meaning of social entrepreneurship.

The field of social entrepreneurship has sparked a great deal interest over the past decade, although much of the research has often been skewed towards the non-profit and public policy sectors. However, the concept of social entrepreneurship encompasses a wide range of activities, including socially conscious individuals and entrepreneurs committed to having a positive impact in society; socially motivated business ventures focused on creating shareholder value while also creating social value in the communities they serve; non-profit organizations applying lessons learned from the business world to cultivate and forge partnerships to have a stronger and scalable social impact; and high net worth individuals supporting a specific social cause or causes through their own foundation or through other social platforms.

Social Entrepreneurship Defined

The terms social entrepreneur and social entrepreneurship were first used by H. Bowen in 1953 in his book *Social Responsibilities of the Businessman,* which introduced business ethics and social responsibility as foundational for businesses and business leaders. The term social entrepreneurship was later popularized in the 1980s by Bill Drayton, founder and CEO of Ashoka, who is often referred to as the Father of Social Entrepreneurship (by the way, I was thrilled to have Bill as one of the interviewees for my research and will expand on our discussion in a later chapter). The definition of social entrepreneurship has evolved further over the past few decades through various research studies. The term has become more expansive, in that it includes innovative activities that create social value that can occur within or across the non-profit, business, and public sectors (Austin, Stevenson, & Wei-Skillern, 2006). Mair and Marti (2006) expanded on the definition of social entrepreneurship as a means to catalyze social change and address social problems by combining resources and applying creativity and innovation in pursuit of social reform. Social enterprises that operate as non-profit organizations are considered tax-exempt or charitable, meaning they do not pay income tax on the money that they receive or the revenue they generate. Typically, they reinvest all donations and net earnings back into the organization to promote social change.

As recently as a decade ago, social entrepreneurship was considered a new phenomenon; however, social entrepreneurial and non-profit organizations have become important structures that deliver services to parts of society that governments fail to reach and that markets choose to ignore (Salamon & Anheier, 1998). They attempt to drive societal transformations by identifying social issues and then galvanizing the community, like-minded partners, industry leaders, and the government sector to address systemic issues.

A social enterprise can operate in various forms, the most prevalent being (1) building the capacity to solve a broad set of social issues; (2) developing products or services to tackle specific social problems; and/or (3) championing advocacy to tackle a specific topic of public interest in order to change policy. To appreciate the framework and construct of a social enterprise, it is helpful to understand where it intersects with other forms of business ventures.

As Figure 1 illustrates, between the two primary forms of business ventures – traditional for-profit and traditional non-profit businesses – there are hybrid business ventures that include non-profit social enterprises and for-profit social enterprises. Social entrepreneurship is a form of business venture that may include for-profit businesses with a social mission as well as social non-profit businesses that may partially rely on their own revenue stream to fund their programs and platforms. Hence, a social enterprise can operate in various forms, with the primary goal of creating social value and having an impact through activities that include building the capacity to solve a broad set of social issues; developing products or services to tackle specific social problems; and advocacy to tackle a specific topic or set of topics of public interest in order to affect policy change.

Figure 1. Forms of Business Ventures

In the current business environment, with enhanced social and environmental awareness, firms are expected to increase shareholder value through profits while also increasing social value by promoting corporate social responsibility. When an enterprise is formed as a social entrepreneurial firm, a deliberate decision is made to integrate social consciousness into the business model, incorporating the goals of revenue generation, social awareness, and impact, with environmental considerations.

Whether the emergence of the social entrepreneurial model results from personal consciousness to pursue social responsibility or increased public awareness and pressure to demand social and environmental responsibilities from corporations, social entrepreneurship has been viewed as a business model with a continuum of objectives ranging from a purely social mission through combinations of social and profit motives. Clearly, the definition of social entrepreneurship has evolved over time. I personally like the definition put forth by Austin, Stevenson, and Wei-Skillern (2006), who defined social entrepreneurship as innovative social value creating activities that can occur within or across the non-profit, business, and public sectors. However, social entrepreneurship is best enabled by the innovative and pattern-breaking individuals that comprise them. This is why I feel it is also important to understand the leadership characteristics of a social entrepreneur that extend beyond those of the traditional entrepreneur. Social entrepreneurs embody greater empathy, emotional intelligence, and selflessness, and are driven by a stronger moral compass and sense of obligation to serve society and humanity at large. More on this in Chapters 15–21.

Social entrepreneurs and enterprises play an important role in the social change framework, as shown in Figure 2, which places global and social needs and opportunities at its center. Social entrepreneurs develop social enterprises to deal with these social needs and opportunities of varying scales. They do so by finding sources for and raising money and collaborating with partners and stakeholders. The outcome of a successful social enterprise ultimately results in the resolution of social issues and establishes a framework for lasting and sustainable change.

Figure 2. **Social Change Framework**

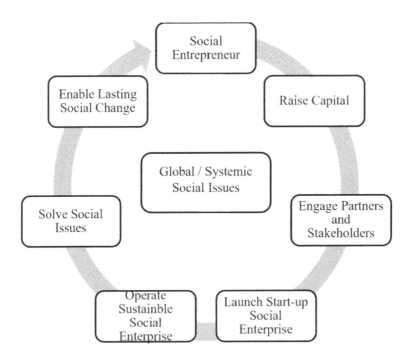

Social entrepreneurship is often mistaken for Corporate Social Responsibility (CSR), a phenomenon that has also gained popularity in the business world over the past few decades. CSR, a broad term that describes corporate citizenship, corporate social involvement or community, and corporate philanthropy, helps firms fulfill their economic and social responsibilities, ensuring the well-being and social welfare of the community.

CSR brings many benefits and can be an important factor in supporting social entrepreneurship, but it does not cover the breadth of social entrepreneurship. Social entrepreneurship encompasses the use of resources to create benefits for society. The social entrepreneur is the person who seeks to benefit society through innovation and risk taking. Thus, social entrepreneurship is the field that concentrates on solving social problems in more focused, organized, sustainable, and scalable ways.

The Life Cycle of a Social Entrepreneur

Applying the social change framework to a social enterprise reveals the journey of social entrepreneurs through key stages of their entrepreneurship lifecycle. As Figure 3 illustrates, my analysis identified four primary stages in the lifecycle of a social entrepreneur: entering, launching, operating, and exiting.

Figure 3. **The Life Cycle of a Social Entrepreneur**

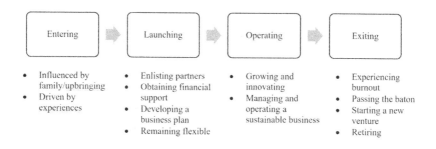

A social entrepreneur's decision to enter the field of social entrepreneurship often begins early in life and is driven by factors including family influence, his/her environment, experiences, and networks. These factors instill a moral compass in the individual, generally starting early in life. Launching a social enterprise requires enlisting and collaborating with partners and stakeholders in order to obtain moral, financial, and operational support. Determining when the timing is right to launch a social enterprise requires a multi-pronged approach. First, the entrepreneur must select a location to launch the enterprise, based on a gap between the supply of and demand for the product or service and the existence of the required infrastructure. They must establish the vehicles to raise awareness, acceptance, and accessibility of support; and collaborate with the government, companies, partners, foundations, and stakeholders to build capacity for lasting change.

Operating a social enterprise creates various tensions, including the widely studied conflict between a social mission and financial results. In fact, the launching and operating stages of a social enterprise are fraught with several competing challenges that are the source of tensions and contradictions and require ongoing balancing and management on the part of the social entrepreneur. If not managed and mitigated adequately, these tensions and contradictions can lead to the failure of a social enterprise and result in the exit of a social entrepreneur from the enterprise and/or from the field of social entrepreneurship altogether. A social entrepreneur may also choose to exit a social enterprise due to burnout and exhaustion, retirement, or to cede the helm to a successor and go on to launch a new social enterprise.

Commercial enterprises typically go through the phases of birth, growth, maturity, decline, and reemergence of the entrepreneurial ecosystem. The life cycle of a traditional entrepreneur can also be described as preparation, embarkation, exploration, exploitation, and transformation. This life cycle theory has also been examined to describe the process of change in organizations. The theory posits that change is inevitable and that the organization must adapt to change accordingly to progress through the stages of evolution.

It is interesting to note that unlike traditional entrepreneurs, I found that social entrepreneurs are inseparable from the enterprise. Therefore, the life cycle of a social enterprise is a direct reflection of the life cycle of a social entrepreneur. In fact, social entrepreneurs do not view their enterprise as a typical business but rather as a vehicle to advance their social mission. They are driven by passion over profit, and they define success in terms of social value over economic value. Further, they view the concept of life cycle not as a finite and prescribed process, but rather as a continuum marked by ongoing change and evolution. This view enables them to adapt, innovate, and mold themselves and their enterprise and to evolve during their journey versus working towards achieving a singular pre-established goal and considering that their work is done upon the achievement of that goal.

Social Impact Measurement

Despite the focus on CSR in business enterprises and the popularity of social entrepreneurship over the past few decades, measuring social and environmental value has proven elusive. The phrase "Triple Bottom Line" (TBL) was first coined by Elkington in 1994 as a framework that incorporates three dimensions of organizational performance: financial, social, and environmental. Savitz (2006) defined TBL as a measure that encapsulates sustainability in terms of the organization's contributions in the areas of profitability, shareholder value, and social, human, and environmental value. Today, the TBL dimensions are also commonly called the three Ps: People, Planet, and Profits. However, well before Elkington introduced the TBL sustainability concept and Savitz defined it, academic scholars and environmentalists had wrestled with a framework for and measurement of social value and sustainability.

Although TBL lacks a common unit of measure and supporting data for calculating an organization's contributions to sustainability, the framework allows organizations to evaluate the ramifications of their decisions from a more holistic and long-term perspective. This limitation extends to the social sector, as social entrepreneurs and enterprises continue to struggle to come up with a quantifiable measure of social value creation. Further, the primary goals of a traditional organization are generally driven by the need to create shareholder value and therefore, are focused on revenue, market share, margins, net income, and other financial metrics that are both quantifiable and easily measurable over specific periods – monthly, quarterly, and annually. On the other hand, the goals of a social enterprise are often complex in that they tend to focus on a broad impact on a community or social change and are often long-term in nature. Therefore, the results may be evident only over several years and perhaps over decades.

There are two primary limitations in measuring social value – lack of quantitative data and lack of a methodology. Social value creation is also difficult to quantify and measure as it often includes the alignment and collaboration across various sectors and groups – community, economic, socio-political, public policy, and advocacy. Communicating its value proposition to investors or funders, donors, partners, volunteers, and other stakeholders becomes a significant challenge for a social entrepreneur. Since investment capital providers generally seek metrics-based returns and results as measures of success, social enterprises, as well as servant leaders who head such enterprises, are often limited in their ability to innovate and experiment and therefore, are stifled in their ability to have a social impact.

Funding Model and Impact Investment Capital

Funding for social enterprises can come from a number of sources, including grants and funding from the government and its agencies; private sector donations from sources such as individual donors, for-profit organizations, foundations, and non-profit organizations; revenue generated from the sale of its own products or services; and social impact investment capital from public sector investors and organizations that are committed to putting their capital to use for the benefit of society with the expectation of a return on their investment. Given that some funders often predicate the allocation of their donations or investments on performance against set expectations, the amount of impact capital may fluctuate and be less consistent and reliable. In addition, in down market cycles, these donations tend to dry up.

The primary purpose of impact investment capital is to have a social and environmental impact that responds to the social needs of a community, with the expectation of earning a financial return on the investment. This approach is different from a donation or grant that is made for charitable purposes with no expectation of a financial return. The need to achieve an investment return in this context gives rise to the concept of "blended value," which combines the value generated from three elements: economic, social, and environmental. Blended value is more than the sum of the parts of this triple bottom line. It is the recognition that capital, community, and commerce can create more together than the sum of the three elements independently.

Though there has been some progress made in the area of impact investing in recent years, attracting such capital still comes with numerous challenges. First, there continues to be a stigma attached to impact investing because it presumes below-market financial returns. Second, there is underlying skepticism about the ability of an enterprise to attract impact capital to pursue and prioritize sustainable social change. Third, impact investment can often come with a quid pro quo to promote the investor's personal interests or agenda, which risks misaligning and distracting from the intended goal of the mission. Finally, societal biases and cultural barriers can limit access to impact capital for women and minority social entrepreneurs.

Environmental, Social, and Governance (ESG) investing has become a popular vehicle that promotes the focus on sustainability and social responsibility. ESG investing can have social benefits by providing access to an important source of funding in social entrepreneurship, a hedge against disasters and shocks related to the climate, and protection against environment-related regulatory changes. However, it typically yields lower expected returns and therefore, is not always viewed as an attractive instrument by investors.

While there are important contextual, structural, and financial considerations in launching and operating a social enterprise, social value creation at scale is often the result of co-creation and collaboration between and among social entrepreneurs and enterprises, business leaders and companies, volunteers, partners, communities, governments, and society at large. As noted above, the mission and strategy of a social enterprise are strongly affected by its ability to attract impact investment capital. Therefore, the reliance on the need to raise capital becomes an important limiting factor in the entrepreneur's ability to launch and operate a social enterprise.

CHAPTER 1:

BALANCING TENSIONS AND TRADE-OFFS

It is widely acknowledged that there is an inherent underlying conflict that social entrepreneurs experience by virtue of achieving two goals simultaneously: the social mission and financial goals of the enterprise. Smith (2015) expanded on these social-financial tensions using four organizational theories: (1) institutional theory, meaning the tensions related to the relationship between the organization and the environment; (2) organizational identity theory, meaning the tensions related to the organization's belonging in the community; (3) stakeholder theory, meaning the tensions related to addressing the demands of multiple stakeholders; and (4) paradox theory, meaning the overall tensions between the social mission and the business purpose of the enterprise. Some management of multiple organizations face social mission design tensions during the initial stage of an enterprise, that later shift to tensions among various social goals and having to make choices about which goals to pursue and which ones to defer or abandon. However, in addition to the financial and mission design tensions, social entrepreneurs encounter other challenges during the life cycle of their social enterprise, the most recurring challenges being the lack of capital and funding, the inability to attract talent, the lack of government support, and the allocation and mobilization of limited financial and human resources.

Goyal, Sergi, and Jaiswal (2015) referred to these as "multi-dimensional challenges" as causing dilemmas for social entrepreneurs. These dilemmas can arise due to the general environment and infrastructure that social entrepreneurs face, such as gaps in income, education, and healthcare, and having to align partners, investors, competitors, and the government. In addition, ethical dilemmas can also arise driven largely by the dual goals of making a social impact and rewarding shareholders. Other issues include a general lack of information and trust in the social enterprise or a general lack of financial and human resources in the social sector. The need to align the social goals and investors' expectations can prove challenging, as well as the need to align the differing interests of various partners and stakeholders. Finally, ethical dilemmas can arise from the need to establish the trust, credibility, and relevance of the social enterprise while balancing its impact, financial, and growth objectives.

Several scholars have previously noted that social entrepreneurs have the ability to balance the often-conflicting social mission and financial goals; however, others have indicated that social entrepreneurs face other multi-dimensional tensions in trying to achieve these conflicting goals. These multi-dimensional tensions can be grouped into three primary categories that are related to the mission (conflict between which goals to pursue), the people (conflict between divergent views of key stakeholders), and the results (conflict between pursuing short-term versus long-term results).

Previous studies on social entrepreneurs have primarily addressed the tension between having a social impact and achieving financial results. Zhu, Rooney, and Phillips (2013) introduced a practice-based wisdom approach to address these competing social welfare and commercial success goals in social entrepreneurship. They established that social welfare logic is the fundamental foundation of social enterprises, but commercial logic is also needed to ensure the financial sustainability of the enterprise.

Pache and Chowdhury (2012) discussed these "competing institutional logics" and added a "public sector logic" that focuses on "ensuring fairness and transparency across different levels of society" (p. 498). These tensions exist in all social enterprises and pose the greatest challenges for social entrepreneurship. In order to manage and overcome these challenges, Pache and Chowdhury (2012) suggested "bridging" these logics by raising awareness and understanding and assessing the impacts of these logics on the enterprise and its various stakeholders (p. 501).

Smith and Lewis (2011, p. 382) referred to these tensions as paradoxes that are "contradictory, yet integrated elements that exist simultaneously and persist over time." This inherent paradox of pursuing a social mission using a business framework leads to ongoing competing demands and prioritization of social and financial objectives. As a result, this paradox creates tensions and conflicts for social entrepreneurs and leads to the development of certain unique characteristics and traits in social entrepreneurs that are required to manage these tensions and conflicts.

My research delved deeper into the social enterprise's mission, operating framework, reliance on stakeholders, and volunteers, and the inherent idealistic traits of the social entrepreneur in order to identify several other critical tensions that social entrepreneurs face. These tensions require a social entrepreneur to perform a balancing act on a routine basis as coping mechanisms to deal with these conflicts and misalignments. As Figure 4 illustrates, I have grouped these tensions into six categories: existential, moral, inertial, structural, relational, and aptitudinal.

Figure 4. **Balancing Tensions and Trade-offs**

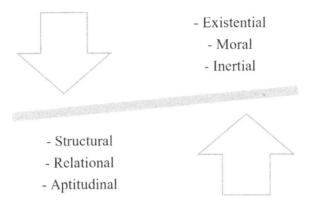

These tensions include having to balance the need for personal financial security while advancing the mission of the social enterprise (existential tension); pursuing the moral obligation to do good with the roadblocks that are often faced in that journey (moral tension); empowering partners and volunteers who have inertial mindsets (inertial tension); achieving short-term incremental change, while also simultaneously laying the foundation for a long-term systemic impact (structural tension); relying on multiple stakeholders who have divergent and potentially misaligned interests (relational tension); and balancing the often idealistic traits of a social entrepreneur with the need to be realistic and pragmatic (aptitudinal tension). The succeeding chapters expand on the multiple tensions and trade-offs that a social entrepreneur must balance in launching and operating a social enterprise.

CHAPTER 2

EXISTENTIAL TENSION – MONEY VS MISSION

Social entrepreneurs take on the difficult challenge of launching and operating financially sustainable businesses that are primarily focused on solving social problems for the greater good of society and humanity. However, they face an existential tension caused by the need to achieve personal and familial security before pursuing social entrepreneurship. This existential tension exists throughout their social entrepreneurial journey and extends to their constant need to balance the tension between social and financial goals. This ongoing conflict creates the risk of the enterprise either losing its focus on its social mission or jeopardizing its financial existence as a sustainable and enduring enterprise.

As validated by nearly all social entrepreneurs that I spoke with, an adequate level of personal and familial financial security is essential before a social entrepreneur can dedicate him or herself to social impact. A case in point, Roshan Paul co-founded Amani Institute in 2011, along with a colleague, Iliana Rabbat, and served as its CEO till 2021, and continues to serve on its board of directors. The Amani Institute, which was founded in Kenya and later expanded to Brazil and India, is dedicated to helping individuals and organizations build the skills they need to solve social problems across the world.

Roshan grew up in Bangalore, India, with a middle-class upbringing, and with parents who encouraged him to pursue his passion, as long as he could support himself. His higher education in the USA exposed him to liberal arts and initially, he considered conventional career paths, such as investment banking or management consulting. However, Roshan's perspective shifted due to significant global events, such as the 9/11 attack in the USA in 2001 and the Gujarat riots in India in 2002. These events made him reevaluate his career choices and question the impact he wanted to make in this world. Roshan decided to decline job offers in the private sector and returned to India to pursue social entrepreneurship. About a decade later, Roshan co-founded The Amani Institute with the goal of bridging the gap in social entrepreneurship education by offering practical training and skills development to individuals to enable them to pursue meaningful careers in social entrepreneurship.

Roshan spoke of the financial struggles of pursuing social entrepreneurship and the personal sacrifices made by him and his colleagues to keep themselves and their social enterprise afloat. He spoke of them maintaining two full-time jobs and burning the candle at both ends for several years, while they were simultaneously launching and establishing The Amani Institute. Fortunately, with their hard work, long hours, and the support of their personal and professional networks, they were able to survive and thrive during this critical period.

Similarly, the need for a social enterprise's financial and economic survival trumps the scope and timeliness of the achievement of its social mission. Several social entrepreneurs noted that in order to obtain funding, meeting the funders' needs became their top priority. The enterprise's social mission often took a back seat. All of the social entrepreneurs acknowledged the importance of capital, the difficulty in growing and scaling the enterprise, and making an impact without sufficient financial resources. While they all spoke passionately about being motivated by the social mission rather than financial returns, they acknowledged that favoring money versus the mission is necessary for the social enterprise to survive.

This push for survival often leads to the social entrepreneur having to pivot the mission and/or operating model of the enterprise. For example, Roshan and Iliana's initial vision was to have The Amani Institute be a university support organization, rather than a separate entity. In fact, they explored partnerships with 30–40 universities in the USA and Europe, but due to the significant challenges they faced, they decided to structure The Amani Institute as a standalone organization. This adaptive approach allowed them to pivot their vision and operating model to achieve financial resilience and enabled them to expand from their base in Kenya to Brazil and India. Several years later, when the COVID-19 global pandemic hit, they were able to pivot again to virtual programming while maintaining their personalized, high-touch approach.

In summary, existential tensions at the personal level involve the need to achieve personal and familial financial security as a priority while also pursuing a career in social entrepreneurship. Similarly, existential tensions at the organizational level involve the need to constantly balance the social and financial goals of an enterprise. This creates a paradox of sorts for social entrepreneurs, and acknowledging and accepting this paradox can lead a social entrepreneur to develop innovative yet practical alternatives that can be the difference between the survival and failure of a social enterprise.

CHAPTER 3:

MORAL TENSION –
DUTY VS DOUBT

Social entrepreneurs face moral tension by having a strong sense of moral obligation to add social value to society, while also becoming somewhat cynical in the face of the many ongoing challenges they encounter. Moral obligation is an outgrowth of having a stronger moral compass that results from being able to differentiate right from wrong, good from evil, selflessness from selfishness, and embracing the duty and responsibility to help those in need. This strong moral compass can result from one's upbringing, environment, or specific individuals or events that help shape an individual's desire to pursue social entrepreneurship.

Tiwari, Bhat, and Tikoria (2017) provided an additional definition of moral obligation as a "metaphysical commitment" that results in positive action for the greater good. In the social entrepreneurial context, moral obligation drives the social entrepreneur's strong commitment and sense of obligation to solving social problems and the ability to balance the social and profit imperatives. However, I found that a moral tension exists between the strong will of the social entrepreneurs' desire to solve social problems and the limitations they encounter in trying to realize their goals. My informants attributed their deep sense of moral obligation to factors such as a strong sense of self and their panoramic view of society and the world and how they fit into it. They spoke of being drawn to the social sector by their internal compass and personal values of wanting to live their lives with purpose. They felt they could make a difference in people's lives, promote wisdom and compassion among humanity, and wanted to make a mark on the world.

One of my informants, Indira Kumar, has dedicated her life to social service, both in the USA and in her hometown in Guyana, South America. Her most recent social venture is Global Economic Foundation, which was established with an aim to help and create a sustainable life for all needy people, including refugees, individuals in asylums, and low-income immigrants. The Foundation is dedicated to bringing new approaches to solving systemic, socio-economic problems faced by this under-served population in the USA.

Indira's motivation for social work stems from her exposure to poverty and suffering in various countries and is deeply engrained in her personal values and beliefs. She spoke of her admiration for Mother Teresa and belief in selfless giving. She spoke with great humility about the village in Guyana where she grew up and her desire to help improve today's living conditions and the lives of children in her village. She also spoke of her strong sense of moral responsibility and duty to serve others, being the oldest of eight siblings in her family.

However, I sensed a great degree of exhaustion and weariness when she spoke of the challenges she has had to face in order to stay afloat and how extremely difficult her social entrepreneurial journey has been. One of her social ventures came close to shutting down due to the COVID-19 pandemic but managed to barely stay afloat due to her and other volunteers' persistence and perseverance. In closing, she also expressed great sadness and disappointment with others who have achieved great wealth and success in life and don't do more for their community and society at large.

Experiences such as this can make social entrepreneurs cynical about their ability to fulfill their social mission and make a lasting impact. Several informants spoke of the need for institutional survival versus being inherently good. They even distinguished between good and bad social entrepreneurship. Some noted that, sometimes, creating social value may lead to a social evil, in that, solving a social problem may lead to the creation of new problems in society.

Another informant spoke of the Rumpelstiltskin syndrome, describing the power of a name in social entrepreneurship versus its social cause or mission, that sometimes leads them to make unrealistic demands and set unachievable expectations of themselves and others. Many informants expressed their skepticism about national and global politics and infrastructure leading to the need to explore hybrid models of social impact when that time could be spent on solving social problems and enabling social change. Other challenges included high expectations from investors, misalignment with, and lack of support from partners and stakeholders. These challenges were often at odds with the social entrepreneur's sense of moral obligation to make a social impact. These factors often create a sense of cynicism between the social entrepreneur's strong sense of moral obligation and duty towards humanity with the reality of not being able to fulfill their mission in the face of ongoing struggles.

Another informant expressed cynicism about social entrepreneurs being good-hearted but unskilled in getting the work done. As a result, they may tend to accept mediocrity, leading to the image of social enterprises as well-meaning but "inept beggars." In summary, while social entrepreneurs are typically motivated by their strong moral obligation to give back to society, they can become cynical over time due to their relentless and often unsuccessful attempts to enlist support from others, resulting in their continuous push for personal and institutional survival. Hence, they begin to question the efficacy of their social enterprise and their ability to realize its mission.

CHAPTER 4:

INERTIAL TENSION – APATHY VS ACTION

All the social entrepreneurs I interviewed spoke of inertial tensions as being rooted in several factors. First, the reliance on funders, partners, and stakeholders requires aligning their goals with those of the social enterprise, which is often extremely difficult to achieve. The time and energy spent in trying to do so results from inertia and apathy on the part of these actors, taking the focus away from the social mission of the enterprise. This effort often leads to the fragmentation and dilution of the enterprise's mission and may require the enterprise to change and adapt to make forward progress. Consequently, the reformulation of the enterprise's social mission, goals, and objectives, the delay and deferral of key initiatives, and the focus on resources and stakeholder alignment caused by stakeholder apathy can lead to organizational inertia, hence impeding the progress towards mission fulfillment.

Second, attracting and recruiting mission-oriented and mission-aligned individuals to come on board in lower paying jobs in a resource-starved industry often leads to inertia and delays. One informant described having to settle for the best person he could afford versus hiring the best person for the job. Recruiting top talent is an ongoing challenge for the social sector due to the inability to compete with the marketplace. Further, social enterprises seek to hire professionals who want to live lives of significance and purpose. Unfortunately, that desire does not always equate to hiring and being able to afford an individual who has the skills and competencies necessary for the job. This issue creates inertial tension for social entrepreneurs driven by the conflict between their passion and desire to make progress and the limitations they face in hiring those who have the skills to make their vision a reality.

Third, the operational challenges of running and operating a social enterprise can also lead to inertial tensions for social entrepreneurs. Several informants described being distracted by having to deal with personnel-related issues, such as recruitment, retention, compensation, and performance management. They also lacked the business, operational, and managerial skills to run the organization. Such tensions, coupled with operating with a limited budget in a resource-constrained environment, dealing with the stress of making payroll, having to lay off staff during financial downturns, and taking on administrative duties and assignments, led to inertial tensions, causing mission paralysis, which took the focus away from the social goals of the enterprise.

Finally, the fundraising and governance aspects of a social enterprise were also noted as a cause of inertial tension. Several informants mentioned the capital-raising component of their jobs as being the most critical and time-consuming of all. They also spoke of the challenge of managing the frequent and ongoing changes in the board's composition and leadership, resulting in the need to provide orientation, onboarding, and training to the board on a regular basis. One informant indicated that the ongoing turnover of their board's leadership also had a negative impact on the enterprise's performance and achievement of its mission, as the entrepreneur is always several steps ahead of the board and must spend time and effort to educate the board and gain alignment instead of focusing on achieving the social enterprise's mission and vision.

My conversation with Nicolas (Nick) Cuttriss provided an example of inertial tension. Nick is the Co-Founder and Board Chairman of AYUDA (American Youth Understanding Diabetes Abroad) since 1995. Since its inception, AYUDA, a non-profit organization, has empowered American youth to serve as agents of change for children with diabetes in communities overseas. Nick's journey into social entrepreneurship began in high school when Nick and his friend Jesse Fuchs-Simon encountered a child, Jose Gabriel, in Quito, Ecuador, with Type 1 diabetes and lacked access to proper care due to financial constraints. Jose, a six-month-old child, had gone into a coma and despite the efforts of his parents, both of whom were physicians, could not get healthy. They spent most of the family's income on insulin for Jose but to no avail. A few years later, Jose lapsed into another coma; with no other options available to his family, they brought Jose to the USA for treatment. As teenagers, Nick and Jesse came to realize that the lack of diabetes education can be just as dangerous to children's lives as the lack of insulin. They didn't know much about diabetes at that time but were driven by the desire to help. With limited resources, they began creating educational materials for children with diabetes and found that their own youth and the relatability of their message were powerful in engaging other young people in their mission. After obtaining some seed money, they launched AYUDA in Ecuador and then expanded it to other parts of Latin America and the world. As the organization grew, they formed partnerships with local organizations and healthcare providers in different countries in order to establish various programs and initiatives.

Nick described the challenges they faced during the start-up phase, including navigating the politics and dynamics in different countries, learning to choose the right partners, and dealing with corruption bureaucracy. These roadblocks slowed their progress and required careful navigation and persistence in building trust while remaining true to their core values. He also credits experiential learning and mentorships from various individuals, including family, friends, and colleagues for helping him overcome these challenges.

Other social entrepreneurs also described inertial tension resulting in mission drift due to various factors. Examples include inertia and the lack of alignment on the part of funders, partners, and stakeholders; challenges with the recruitment and retention of talent; operational challenges; governance turnover and friction; and a plethora of operational challenges that divert a social entrepreneur's focus away from the enterprise's mission. Launching and operating a social enterprise requires working with many external partners and stakeholders who may have competing goals and expectations regarding the social mission and the economic goals of the social enterprise. Many of these collaborative and collective efforts require enlisting volunteers who donate their time to support a cause that they are interested in. Such efforts can be community-oriented initiatives or larger-scale systemic initiatives that require cross-sector and even cross-country support. Co-creation through collective social entrepreneurship is often necessary to successfully solve social issues at the community and environmental levels by enlisting cooperation and support from a diverse group of participants. However, reliance on multiple partners, stakeholders, and volunteers often results in divergent views and agendas, leading to inertia, mission fragmentation, or mission drift.

Previous research on social entrepreneurship has also focused on the relationship between the enterprise and the employees in the pursuit of its social mission. These studies have investigated the internal conflicts that may occur in the social enterprise resulting from the fragmented alignment of its employees with either the enterprise's social or financial goals, driven by their own personal values and interests. These internal conflicts can have a negative impact on the organization's productivity and performance, and achievement of its goals.

To summarize, inertial tension can result from apathy on the part of external stakeholders with differing opinions, goals, and expectations and internal employees who may have divergent views regarding the enterprise's mission. Inertial tension can also occur on a larger scale, meaning a community, region, or country's unwillingness or lack of readiness to coalesce in order to tackle a systemic social issue. Social entrepreneurs may have excellent ideas for tackling societal challenges but are often unable to take action or take swift action because they are impeded by the lack of support from the various stakeholders.

CHAPTER 5:

STRUCTURAL TENSION – MODEL VS METHOD

Many social entrepreneurs described various tensions during the launch and operating phases of a social enterprise that I have classified as structural tensions. Such tensions are related to the overall business framework and operating model of the social enterprise. Social entrepreneurs must deal with structural tensions that are caused by several factors. The first factor results from the development of an idea or concept for the launch. Several informants spoke of the dilemma between developing a top-down conceptual theory of change and seeking financial support to execute against it versus developing a bottom-up proof of concept in order to market the idea to funders and stakeholders. On the one hand, the informants noted that a theory of change is necessary and must first be developed and shared with investors and stakeholders before investing significant resources in developing a detailed business plan. On the other hand, they also emphasized the need to develop a minimally viable product or a proof of concept with a business and marketing plan to pitch to investors, donors, and stakeholders.

The second factor is the need to remain flexible and the willingness to include input from funders and stakeholders, while also having a fine-tuned business plan to seek investment capital. Several social entrepreneurs discussed the many stresses and frustrations that they faced in launching their social enterprises. Several informants emphasized that they plunged into their enterprise without even knowing what launching actually meant and trusting that the rest would follow. Thus, they were perpetually in discovery mode and were figuring out the rules and process along the way. As a result, they had to be flexible enough to constantly test and refine their goals and processes based on direct market, investor, and consumer feedback. Using the popular phrase "if you build it, they will come," one informant said that social entrepreneurs often rely on trust and faith when they launch a social enterprise.

Previous studies on social entrepreneurship have introduced concepts that relate to the structural construct of a social enterprise. Garud, Jain, and Tuertscher (2008) created the concept of being "incomplete by design," noting that achieving completeness is not realistic in an environment that is marked by continuous change. In such situations, a practical approach must be utilized to deal with incompleteness in a creative, yet productive manner.

The third factor involves the goal-setting process of the social enterprise. Social entrepreneurs must choose whether to seek an aspirational goal or one that is somewhat limited based on what is in their control and within their existing parameters and constraints. The informants described this struggle between establishing aspirational and long-term social goals versus developing more practical and short-term goals based on existing limitations as being a fundamental structural constraint for them during the launch and operational phases of their social enterprises.

Sarasvathy (2001) provided two frames for decision-making in developing goals for an enterprise – causation and effectuation. The causation frame leads to developing goals that are predictive, deliberate, and pre-determined. On the other hand, the effectuation frame leads to developing goals based on what is available and within the control of the social entrepreneur. Causation processes start with a set of given options regarding goals and lead to the selection of the desired goals for the enterprise. On the other hand, effectuation processes start with a set of assumptions and boundaries that are within the entrepreneur's control and lead to the selection of the desired goals within those parameters and limitations. Sarasvathy also stated that enterprises that use the effectuation frame for goal setting are likely to be more successful and likely to fail early if they do fail, due primarily to the greater degree of pragmatism and control that is applied in the goal-setting process.

Zahra and Wright (2016) argued that social entrepreneurs must focus on the achievement of "blended value" in the start-up and growth phases of an enterprise by focusing on financial, social, and environmental value creation that benefits society. Battilana et al. (2015) also noted that having social and financial objectives causes conflicts and inconsistencies for social entrepreneurs.

Finally, structural tensions are inherent in social enterprises due to the ongoing conflict between the need to fundraise and finance the organization versus focusing on the achievement of its social mission. My informants described their ongoing search for capital – investment funding and revenue generation – as being the most difficult and an all-consuming aspect of their jobs. They also admitted that the focus on raising capital detracted from their ability to solve social problems, but it was critical for the launch, growth, and sustainability of their enterprise.

There is an inherent paradox in the attempt to pursue a social mission through business means, which leads to the emergence of competing demands related to social and financial objectives. A paradox in management refers to unified, yet contradictory factors that exist concurrently and continue over time. This paradox manifests itself in the central characteristics of social enterprises and creates several tensions for social entrepreneurs. First, social entrepreneurs must collaborate with multiple stakeholders with competing interests and expectations regarding financial performance and the pursuit of the social mission. Second, social entrepreneurs often pursue conflicting goals, such as short-term financial goals versus goals involving a longer-term social impact. Finally, social entrepreneurs often engage in inconsistent activities aimed at achieving both financial and social goals. The results can lead to mission drift and limited resources, greatly impeding the enterprise's ability to achieve its mission and goals.

This paradox was best described by Robert Egger, the Founder of DC Central Kitchen. In his interview, Robert shared his background and journey into social entrepreneurship as being greatly influenced by his upbringing and the historical events that shaped his worldview. He spoke of the civil rights movement, the assassination of prominent figures like Dr. Martin Luther King, Jr. and Robert Kennedy, and the power of boycotts as a form of social activism. Robert's initial career involved running nightclubs, where he discovered the potential of using entertainment and creative methods to convey important ideas related to social justice and economics. His entry into social entrepreneurship began in 1988, when he started his first catering company, DC Central Kitchen. This venture aimed to challenge the traditional philanthropic approach to address hunger and homelessness. Robert's approach was to create an entity that could earn its own income and provide jobs and training for marginalized individuals, effectively replacing charity with opportunity.

Since 1988, DC Central Kitchen has become an iconic social enterprise that combats hunger and poverty through job training and job creation. The organization provides culinary job training to individuals, brings nutritious foods to individuals and communities in need, while also creating jobs. In describing the inherent and ongoing structural tension arising from the focus on revenue versus mission, Robert spoke specifically of the need for a new business model to support capital and fundraising, since social entrepreneurship doesn't have the same access to capital that for-profit companies do. He criticized the traditional philanthropy model, suggesting that it doesn't address the root causes of problems and called for a new business model that can reduce the need for charity. He emphasized the importance of using the power of capitalism to drive social change and sees social enterprise as a means to reward and incentivize positive behavior while also providing the needed goods and services. He described the prevalent social entrepreneurship business model as a purposeful design flaw that prevents social entrepreneurs from exerting any economic or political power in the system and challenging the status quo of philanthropy, and that perhaps a new social entrepreneurship business model would diminish the need for charity, as social awareness and objectives would become imbedded in all company's missions.

To recap, structural tension is caused by several other factors that are inherent to social entrepreneurship. During the launch phase of an enterprise, the social entrepreneur must balance the tension between developing a top-down conceptual theory of change that is adaptable to enlist support and ignite excitement among partners and stakeholders versus developing a bottom-up proof of concept and a detailed business plan that is necessary to secure financial funding. Structural tensions also result from the dual and often conflicting focus on achieving the enterprise's short-term financial goals, while also pursuing its long-term social mission and strategic objectives that are focused on the creation of social and environment welfare for society.

CHAPTER 6:

RELATIONAL TENSION – ALLIANCE VS ALIGNMENT

Relational tension arises from the need to engage, enlist, manage, balance, and align with multiple stakeholders throughout the life cycle of a social entrepreneur. Alliances with these stakeholders – funders, institutions, partners, volunteers, and employees – are essential enablers to launching, operating, and growing a social enterprise. Many social entrepreneurs spoke of the lack of support from external sources, such as the government sector, corporations, foundations, and its numerous stakeholders. However, the support that was provided often created alignment tensions due to the alliance and coordination required among several donors having different interests and priorities.

Several social entrepreneurs relayed stories about facing resistance from the government, regulatory issues at the local, state, and federal levels, socio-economic influences including wealth disparities, and the societal changes shaping the motivations of donors, volunteers, and stakeholders. Social entrepreneurs must often work with various stakeholders to address these challenges to achieve their larger social goals.

This tension is exemplified by the experience of Dhananjaya Kumar, the Co-Founder, Chairman, and Trustee of India International School since 1983 and the Co-Founder and CEO of RENEW (Reform Education for a New World) since 2016. India International School is a non-profit educational institution with the mission to provide quality education in the arts, culture, and languages of India; impart the knowledge and skills to younger generations seeking personal growth and harmony with others; and sensitize the youth to basic human values and preservation of the environment. The mission of RENEW is to build a more intelligent, peaceful, and humane society by expanding education to integrate traditional textbook learning with individual growth, social awareness, social welfare, respect for nature, and human values and needs.

Dhananjaya described his early childhood in a rural, agrarian environment in India without modern amenities and how he learned to appreciate and connect with nature. His journey from his early life in the village to his education and career in the USA, which included 25 years as an economist at the World Bank, led him to extensive international travels to many developing countries. He began to question his own life's mission and purpose and developed a strong desire to contribute to the overall welfare of society. He retired early from the World Bank and dedicated his life to exploring new ideas and concepts while advocating for basic education for children's self-development, creativity, and imagination. He emphasized the importance of a multi-disciplinary approach to education and social development and discussed the need for a change in mindsets and assumptions to create a better world for future generations.

Dhananjaya described his many challenges with various stakeholders – including convincing policymakers to consider education reform; finding like-minded individuals who are willing to take on difficult tasks and embrace complexity as necessary steps to bringing about change; encouraging individuals, organizations, and educational institutions to support the global cause of education reform; etc. Working on shifting mindsets to create a multiplier effect while also operating on a day-to-day basis to stay afloat and bringing about slow and incremental change continues to be his mantra, even after 50+ years of dedicating his life to social service.

Despite such fundamental and pervasive misalignment, social entrepreneurs must collaborate with and manage the expectations of these stakeholders. Several social entrepreneurs shared their experiences about being repeatedly denied funding and support. They noted that stakeholder misalignment, including at the board level, posed the most significant challenges for them and often led to feelings of defensiveness and disappointment. My own experiences have shown that social entrepreneurs must invest a great deal of effort in building relationships with their stakeholders, ensuring that their expectations align with the enterprise's mission, and continuously market and sell the social mission and vision of the enterprise.

One social entrepreneur went so far as shifting her role to Communicator-in-Chief from Chief Executive Officer, due to the required focus on relationship building, marketing, selling, negotiating, and building the reputation of the enterprise. Another informant described constantly walking a tightrope in dealing with the different, and often conflicting agendas, egos, and personalities of the various partners, stakeholders, board, and advisors. Nevertheless, all the informants acknowledged their strong reliance on their stakeholder network and the need to combine and leverage their strengths to provide a force for broader and lasting societal change.

As nearly all the social entrepreneurs I spoke with noted, this relational tension between the stakeholder alignment required for the enterprise's survival and the creation of a societal impact, and the realization that it can also lead to the lack of mission focus, resulting in mission fragmentation and dilution, is a double-edged sword that can have positive and negative outcomes. One informant described relational tension as the Achilles' heel of many social entrepreneurs, often requiring them to work the hardest in creating alignment with people who were believed to be the strongest allies and partners.

Given the importance of stakeholders in business and entrepreneurship, this has been a widely researched topic. Freeman (1984) defined stakeholders as individuals or groups who can impact an organization's goals and objectives or are impacted by it. In the commercial sector, stakeholders are often classified into four broad groups: (1) organizational; (2) regulatory; (3) community; and (4) media. These stakeholder groups are also applicable to social entrepreneurship. Organizational stakeholders are directly related to an organization and have the ability to impact its performance. This group typically includes customers, suppliers, employees, shareholders/investors, and other sources of funds, grants, and donations. Regulatory stakeholders include governments, which make environmental regulations; trade associations, which collect information regarding both current and pending legislation; informal networks, which are important sources of technological information; and the firm's competitors, who may become leaders in the social or environmental field through their use of technologies that become industry norms and/or legal mandates. Community stakeholders include community groups, environmental organizations, and other potential lobbying groups. These stakeholders can mobilize public opinion in favor of or against a company. The media is another important stakeholder group. Mass communication technology has changed the role of the media with respect to business. The media can influence society's perceptions of a company, especially when a crisis occurs.

As Schlange (2009) suggested, stakeholders can also be inanimate objects such as the earth or the environment or animate beings such as animals. Therefore, in the broadest sense, stakeholder theory spans across organizational management and ethics, and emphasizes the stakeholders and their relationship with the organization in achieving results that are implicitly driven by value and morals. Burga and Rezania (2016) studied stakeholder theory in social entrepreneurship and mapped "stakeholder salience and stakeholder social issue management valence" to demonstrate the level of misalignment between these two factors.

Contrary to traditional organizations that prioritize stakeholders' needs and emphasize increasing shareholders' value through profit maximization, a stakeholder orientation recognizes that organizations operate within and are accountable to a broad ecosystem, resulting in a shift of perspective that surfaces ethical and societal issues. Companies with a stakeholder orientation view stakeholders as part of an environment that must be managed in order to achieve its social mission. Attention to stakeholder concerns may help an organization achieve greater stakeholder engagement and the support of its strategy and objectives. Given the greater prominence of stakeholders in informing, shaping, and influencing a social enterprise's strategy, innovation, work programs, and execution, it is important to explore the application of a stakeholder orientation in social entrepreneurship.

Based on the nature of a social enterprise's business model, stakeholders play a critical role in the launch and operation of a social enterprise. Nevertheless, although stakeholder management has been a topic of some research in business journals, little empirical research has been done on understanding the effect of a stakeholder orientation and management on social entrepreneurship. Stakeholders often provide funding and support and promote innovation in social enterprises. However, they can also become a source of challenge, due to the conflicting agendas and the lack of alignment between their goals and those of the social enterprise.

Relational tension is a significant obstacle that social entrepreneurs must deal with daily throughout their social entrepreneurial journey. Partners and stakeholders are crucial to social entrepreneurship as enablers who create a multiplier effect. Freeman (1994) described one of the principles of the stakeholder concept as "the principle of who or what really counts" (p. 411).

The strength of collaboration and co-creation among stakeholders can create a social multiplier at the community, regional, and global levels. Zahra and Wright (2016) referred to Silicon Valley as an example of a social multiplier that has enabled the generation of financial capital and other required resources to support the launch of social and commercial enterprises. However, regardless of the scale of certain stakeholders' influence and power, resistance can come from other stakeholders, such as domestic and global forces, regulatory challenges from federal, state, and local governments, socio-economic influences including technological evolution, and general lifestyle shifts affecting donors, volunteers, partners, and competitors in this expanding landscape.

Such resistance is pervasive and results in relational tension for social entrepreneurs. My informants often described this relationship with stakeholders as a double-edged sword, one that was critically important for achieving the enterprise's mission but one that was also extremely difficult to engage, navigate, motivate, and align with the enterprise's mission.

CHAPTER 7:

APTITUDINAL TENSION – RIGHTEOUS VS REALISTIC

Another challenge social entrepreneurs face is aptitudinal tension, which has two aspects. The first is the tension between their idealism in being a righteous entrepreneur and their pragmatism or realism about what they can accomplish. Several informants spoke of their morals and idealism getting in the way of their judgment and realizing that ideology alone is not enough. They must find a way to determine what is practical and achievable. Some informants expressed a great deal of pride in not wanting to be a charity but also discussed the ongoing struggle with the inherent nature of social entrepreneurship as being resource starved. This aptitudinal tension was a constant source of anxiety for social entrepreneurs.

Second, most informants acknowledged being conflicted by the innovation and creativity versus the operational competencies required to launch and run a social enterprise. Several informants spoke of being good visionaries and having the ability to create and sell the vision but having poor operation, business, and people management skills. Those who recognized these shortcomings in themselves often delegated such detailed tasks to others in the organization. One informant said he is fully aware of his strengths and weaknesses. He knows his skills are best suited to being the captain and navigator of the ship but has always hired strong CEOs to steer the ship in the right direction.

My conversation with Burck Smith brought this tension to the forefront. In 1989, Burck founded Smarthinking, one of the first providers of online tutoring. Smarthinking aimed to reshape the traditional labor model in education and move towards a service-based model, leveraging technology capabilities for education delivery. Smarthinking (now a Pearson company) eventually became the foundation for Burck's next venture, StraighterLine, that he launched in 2009. StraighterLine helps colleges offer innovative pathways and programs with the goal of improving enrollment and retention by reducing the cost and risk of pursuing a college degree. It is worth noting that Burck is currently the CEO and founder of Palette Edu, an app that better connects students with the network of adults that support them.

Burck shared his thoughts on the limitations of the current education system, emphasizing the need for a more flexible, adaptable, and individualized approach to learning. He discussed the challenges of redefining education and how technology, particularly online learning, can facilitate this transformation. He highlighted the importance of breaking away from the traditional model and exploring new methods and partnerships to enhance education for students. On the one hand, he showed a great sense of righteousness in his beliefs and actions; however, this was somewhat tempered with his skepticism about the term "social entrepreneurship," suggesting that defining what is truly socially good can be complex and questionable. He believed that the concept is often driven by funder expectations rather than quantifiable social impact metrics. He also questioned the allocation of funds, suggesting that certain initiatives receive attention and funding due to their appeal, whereas other equally valid but less popular initiatives are often left unsupported. Burck went so far as to reflect on the notion that sometimes it becomes difficult to differentiate between good versus bad social entrepreneurship, questioning that an enterprise's social mission and value creation may actually end up leading to social evil, such as in his case, his social enterprise can end up driving some other institutions out of business.

Burck also emphasized the importance of self-awareness and noted that acknowledging personal strengths and weaknesses is crucial. A social entrepreneur is often a visionary, driven by idealism and righteousness who must be adept at creativity, networking, relationship building, storytelling, problem-solving, and adaptability. However, being realistic about establishing social impact goals, financial projections, managing investor expectations, delegating tasks that align with individual strengths, and stepping aside when necessary are all vital aspects of the entrepreneurial journey.

In this context, it is worth noting that the paradox of embeddedness theory (Battilana, 2006) explores the relationship between the institution, human agency, and the individual's social position in understanding how institutional entrepreneurs perform despite institutional pressures. DiMaggio (1988) defined institutional entrepreneurs as entrepreneurs who have sufficient resources to launch enterprises to capitalize on an opportunity that is of interest and value to them. Battilana (2006) defined human agency as an individual's ability to impact the world through their interest in and deliberate pursuit of social issues. The contradiction is in the need for entrepreneurs who are embedded in the institution to distance themselves from the institutional pressures in order to be strategic and innovative. There are two contrasting perspectives with respect to how social enterprises can be run in order to fulfill their social mission. One perspective focuses on the capabilities of the social entrepreneur. The second perspective acknowledges the potential tensions that exist in the organization.

An entrepreneur or the enterprise's founding team often has a deep and lasting impact on the enterprise, such that it can hinder the enterprise's ability and capacity to change and evolve through its business cycle. Boeker (1989) subsequently called this phenomenon "organizational imprinting." Bryant (2014) claimed that the capacity of an enterprise is often shaped by the legacy of the founder's characteristics that are imbedded in that enterprise. He stated that imprinting can be based on three factors: (1) autobiographical, meaning the founder's personal characteristics; (2) transactional, meaning experiences drawn from previous activities; and (3) collective memory, meaning the collective memory of the entrepreneur and the enterprise. These imprinted characteristics become embedded in the enterprise and can persist over time, shaping the organization's structure, culture, brand and identity, stakeholders, partnership networks and relationships, business processes, and cultural norms. While imprinting can stifle progress, it can also be used to improve an enterprise's long-term viability and capacity to adapt by understanding its origin and nature.

Aptitudinal tension is not an area that has been studied previously, as much of the previous research in the field of social entrepreneurship has focused on the heroism of individual entrepreneurs. Studies have explored how they focus simultaneously on the financial and social goals of their enterprise, engage in altruistic activities, and go on to change the world for the better. Social entrepreneurs must balance the aptitudinal tension that emerges from the conflict between their idealistic righteousness and their need to be realistic as well as their aptitude and preference for creativity, innovation, and problem-solving versus running and operating an enterprise.

CHAPTER 8:

SUBSISTING RESPONSES

Why do many social entrepreneurs find it difficult to get off the ground and why do many social enterprises have trouble surviving past the first few years? As described in previous chapters, social enterprises face several challenges, tensions, and trade-offs in launching and operating a social enterprise. These can lead to the difficulty in enlisting a social entrepreneur who models the essential leadership characteristics: forging relationships with partners and stakeholders; developing a quantifiable measure of social value creation; attracting impact investment capital; and establishing a successful and sustainable social enterprise that can demonstrate social value creation over the long term.

There are several existing theories that get to the heart of these questions and provide insights into the challenges and decision-making paradigms that social entrepreneurs use in their enterprises. Bricolage is an outgrowth of being resource constrained, which is a common aspect of social entrepreneurship. Claude Lévi-Strauss, a cultural anthropologist, coined the term "bricoleur" in 1966 to refer to someone who is "a jack-of-all trades" making do with available resources. More recently, in 2010, Di Dominico defined bricolage as an entrepreneur's reaction to resource scarcity and social bricolage as the social entrepreneur's ability to access resources and simply make do with what is available in resource-constrained environments.

As noted earlier, the theory of effectual reasoning is relevant in the start-up and operational stages of a social enterprise, when social entrepreneurs face numerous choices, competing priorities, and conflicting tensions and must make thoughtful and timely decisions. Therefore, it is important to examine their reasoning in the problem-solving and decision-making process. Sarasvathy (2001) stated that "effectuation processes take a set of means as a given and focus on selecting between possible effects that can be created with that set of means" (p. 245). He provided two approaches to an entrepreneur's decision-making process: causation and effectuation. Both begin with the same stated end goal, but causation starts with the "desired results" and effectuation starts with "what is available," that is, who they are, what they know, and who they know. Yusuf (2015) expanded on the research on causation and effectuation. He stated that causation is a methodical, planned, structured process that utilizes an "opportunity-recognition" approach, whereas "effectual problem-solving or decision-making" is used in situations when there is goal ambiguity, anisotropy, and uncertainty.

The concept of imprinting also comes into play in examining how social entrepreneurs cope with the many tensions and trade-offs they face in their entrepreneurial journey. Bryant (2014) claimed that the ability and capacity of an enterprise to change and adapt is often inhibited by the legacy of the founder being imprinted in the enterprise, that can lead to various balancing tensions. However, since imprinting also enables organization wisdom, resulting form collective memory of the entrepreneur and the enterprise, Bryant's research showed that the imprinting process can, in fact, also be used to improve an enterprise's long-term viability.

While previous studies have highlighted the underlying conflicts that social entrepreneurs experience, they have generally focused on the difficulties in achieving two different goals: the social mission and financial goals. Researchers have expanded on this tension to include social mission design tensions (Siegner, Pinkse, & Panwar, 2017). They state that while the tensions between the social and financial goals are more prevalent in the initial stage of an enterprise, they shift to social mission design tensions among various social goals in the later stages of an enterprise. Siegner et al. (2017) also indicated two approaches that social entrepreneurs use to address social mission design tensions – reconciliation strategies and acceptance strategies.

It is helpful to understand the role of social and human capital in addressing the myriad challenges social entrepreneurs face throughout their social enterprises' life cycle. Ferraro (2015) provided a framework for "tackling grand challenges," including "participatory architecture," "multivocal inscription," and "distributed experimentation." Renko (2013) described the challenges of social entrepreneurs in the start-up stage as being driven by the novelty of the products or services being provided; support from the government and stakeholders; the social entrepreneur's personal biases; and the time invested in the venture. Semrau (2015) attributed the ability to address these and other start-up challenges to the entrepreneurs' human capital (derived from education and experience) and social capital (derived from the resources and support provided by the social network structure).

As noted earlier, the paradox of embeddedness theory (Battilana, 2006) uses the relationship between the institution, human agency, and the individual's social position to explain how institutional entrepreneurs perform despite institutional pressures. This research provides two contrasting perspectives on fulfilling social missions effectively. One perspective focuses on the capabilities of the social entrepreneur, whereas the second perspective acknowledges the potential tensions that exist in the business.

According to Smith and Lewis (2011), paradoxes in management refer to elements that are both integrated and conflicting, that coexist and persist over time. Scholars have argued that there is an inherent paradox in the attempt to pursue a social mission through business means, resulting in competing demands related to social and financial objectives. This paradox manifests itself in the characteristics of social enterprises and creates tensions for social entrepreneurs. Social entrepreneurs must collaborate with multiple stakeholders with competing interests and expectations regarding financial performance and the pursuit of the social mission. In addition, social entrepreneurs often pursue conflicting goals, such as short-term financial goals versus having a social impact in the longer term. Finally, social entrepreneurs often engage in inconsistent activities aimed at achieving both financial and social goals. The results can lead to mission drift and limited resources, greatly impeding the enterprise's ability to achieve its mission and goals.

Given these factors, social entrepreneurs must balance multiple tensions and contradictions in the launch and operation of a social enterprise while staying true to their social mission. Figure 5 illustrates the six subsisting responses of social entrepreneurs based on my research.

Figure 5. **Subsisting Responses**

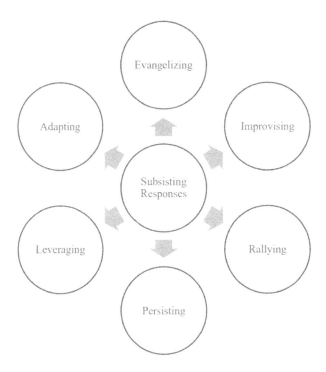

Social entrepreneurs must evangelize to become a disruptive force for lasting change; improvise by making do with the resources that are available; rally tirelessly in order to educate and inspire stakeholders; persist and resist the urge to give up; leverage their personal and professional networks to collaborate and co-create; and adapt by being willing to change and evolve constantly. Each of these subsisting responses are described in further detail in the following chapters.

CHAPTER 9:

EVANGELIZING – BECOMING A DISRUPTIVE FORCE FOR LASTING CHANGE

While working towards advancing the mission of their social enterprise, social entrepreneurs often see themselves as a disruptive force for lasting change. By constantly evangelizing to the various stakeholders, social entrepreneurs create a beacon or a network effect that leads to the creation of a broad, system-wide framework for lasting social change. With their eyes on this ultimate prize, they use evangelizing to manage the moral tensions that arise in launching and operating a social enterprise and are able to cope with short-term setbacks in favor of achieving the long-term social goals of the enterprise and bringing about lasting change in their community and around the world.

Bill Drayton, who is considered the father of social entrepreneurship, is a perfect exemplar of a disruptive force for lasting change. Bill is the Founder and CEO of Ashoka, an organization that he founded in 1980, and has been a pioneering force in the field of social entrepreneurship. Ashoka envisions a world in which everyone is a changemaker. To that end, Ashoka identifies and supports social entrepreneurs around the world and has mobilized a global community of innovative changemakers across the globe.

In my conversation with Bill, he described his background and journey towards social entrepreneurship. He spoke of his upbringing in Manhattan, the influence of his parents, and his early experiences with social and civil rights activism. Bill also spoke of his fascination with India and his trip to India during college which became a transformative experience, as he saw the potential for social entrepreneurship as a means to address social issues. Bill's idea for Ashoka had been brewing since his undergraduate years in college, but he waited until the late 1970s, when he believed the timing was right to develop and launch the organization.

Bill faced significant challenges during the early years of Ashoka. In fact, there wasn't even a word to describe the idea behind Ashoka at that time. Bill knew he had to start with developing a framework for change and building a construct of "social entrepreneurship" that would eventually allow 'everyone' to realize that caring and then organizing to cause change for the good is practical/feasible and respected. He recalled getting 'glassy eyes' from many folks, and others skeptics saying that social entrepreneurship was an 'oxymoron'. Bill also faced challenges in securing funding for Ashoka. In fact, all the funding for the first five years came from individuals or small family foundations, with zero support from institutional foundations as they could not bring themselves to deal with a concept that they had never heard of. These roadblocks never deterred Bill's resolve. Through his persistence and perseverance, he built a strong network and community of individuals who shared his values. As a result, Ashoka's growth has been organic and logical, driven by a commitment to engaging with the whole person, and challenging individuals to see the world in a different way. Over the nearly 45 years since its launch, Ashoka has become a formidable force and movement towards creating a more connected and integrated world where all individuals have the power to bring about positive change. Overall, Bill's social entrepreneurial journey and the growth of Ashoka, which has been the result of his disruptive force to change the prevailing equilibrium, is characterized by a deep commitment to creating a world where everyone can contribute to positive social change.

Like Bill, several other informants spoke of experiences and motivations that extended beyond launching and operating their own social enterprises. They took a broader and more holistic approach to enabling social change through their actions and experiences. They spoke of creating a multiplier effect to promote local, national, and global change. Although through the activities of their enterprises they were attempting to solve a specific social problem, they were also using the platform to create a beacon for future entrepreneurs.

They spoke of actively deploying alumni and other like-minded players to share knowledge and best practices across the globe. In doing so, they hoped to have a dual impact: solving social issues and creating a self-sustaining enterprise, while also creating a model for change by engaging and motivating others to become social changemakers. By developing a vision, inviting the right team, and creating an architecture for social change, social entrepreneurs are able to evangelize across sectors and geographies to see patterns, open doors, and develop frameworks for lasting and ongoing change.

Social entrepreneurs often take great personal risks and use non-linear thinking that is more intention- and intuition-based than data-driven. Bill mentioned that like other social entrepreneurs, he constantly listens for squeaks in the system in order to understand when the world is ready for a solution so that he can take personal action and spark collective action to help give every human being a good life. While listening to the informants as they shared their experiences, I often found it difficult to separate the individual social entrepreneur from the social enterprise. This aspect includes their long-term vision for social change that often extends beyond their short-term social mission and goals. They become evangelists who seek to change mindsets and create a multiplier effect to develop replicable models for change at the local and global levels.

It is this ability and drive to dream beyond the limits of their social enterprises that allows social entrepreneurs to survive despite the various challenges that they must balance on a daily basis. They are able to focus on the bigger picture and view their social enterprise as a means to an end – to develop a framework that enables lasting change. In doing so, they are disrupters who challenge the dominant forces, view themselves as servants of future generations, and focus on who they serve rather than being distracted by challenges and tensions.

Social entrepreneurs are often evangelists who are passionate about their goals and about sharing them with others. This enables them to respond to their ongoing tensions without being consumed by them. Typically, commercial entrepreneurs are driven by autonomy and financial gain as their primary motivations. In contrast, social entrepreneurs are driven by empathy and compassion. As a result, social entrepreneurs have a high degree of entrepreneurial self-efficacy and often set ambitious goals for their enterprises. Their desire to create a framework for lasting social change enables them to keep their eye on this long-term prize and not be distracted by short-term challenges and tensions.

CHAPTER 10:

IMPROVISING – MAKING DO WITH WHAT IS AVAILABLE

All the social entrepreneurs I interviewed shared numerous experiences that highlighted their use of improvisation to cope with and manage the balancing tensions they face in social entrepreneurship. Several informants spoke of experimentation as a standard operating procedure in making the most of what they had. This approach led them to develop creative solutions, internally and with partners, and often take risks, experimenting with the incubation of new ideas, and learning from their successful and failed experiments. Learning by asking questions, active listening, asking for help, trial and error, and reliance on partners helped them transition from scrappy start-ups to thriving and dynamic social enterprises.

Another important demonstration of improvisation comes in the form of social entrepreneurs having to be flexible and agile in their goal setting, planning, and the execution of their day-to-day activities. The informants recounted experiences of having to be nimble and reshaping their business model based on the ebb and flow of capital and being willing to change the company's direction and evolving in order to both survive and to avoid becoming extinct. My research shows that social entrepreneurs are constantly seeking capital and financing. However, due to the lack of success in raising capital, they are forced to improvise and function in resource-constrained environments. Their perpetual lack of resources sparks the need for improvisation, listening to the shifting needs of the stakeholders, and learning from mistakes.

Operating in a resource-constrained environment is synonymous with social entrepreneurship and requires social entrepreneurs to improvise with what they have at their disposal. Making do with the financial and human resources available and being creative through experimentation drives a social entrepreneur to improvise on a continual basis. Improvising helps the social entrepreneur respond to inertial and structural tensions by balancing imperfection with predictability.

Another social entrepreneur that I had the pleasure of speaking with is Tom Dillon, who co-founded The Literacy Lab in 2009, along with his wife, Ashley Johnson. The Literacy Lab provides students with evidence-based and culturally responsive literacy instruction to enable their academic, professional, and personal success. This organization closes the literacy gap by serving students through Grade 3 who are experiencing racial and/or economic inequities by embedding tutors in early childhood centers and elementary schools, in partnership with school districts.

Tom's journey into the field of literacy began when he met his wife, who was a teacher in DC Public Schools. She highlighted the dire literacy issues among her students, and they both decided to address the problem at a larger scale, leading to the launch of their organization. Tom described that his motivation came from three main factors: the shock of witnessing older students unable to read, his problem-solving nature, and his belief that literacy is a fundamental issue and seeing its widespread positive implications if addressed early.

Tom described the process of launching their social enterprise focused on enhancing literacy. They struggled initially and noted that their application for a government program grant that allocated funds for tutoring services was denied. He highlighted the corruption and the lack of oversight in the educational tutoring industry at the time and that many organizations were exploiting these programs. Despite these challenges and through extensive outreach, Tom and Ashley managed to establish a good reputation for their social enterprise for providing quality tutoring services in the DC area. Consequently, they reapplied for the government grant, which was approved, and they were able to secure grants from other philanthropic organizations as well.

Tom noted that the launch of The Literacy Lab was by no means easy and involved several years of hustling and improvising. Throughout the journey, they refused to sacrifice quality over revenue. They struggled with cash flow issues as school districts were slow in making payments. They often had to pay their tutors out of pocket and wait for the delayed payments to be submitted. The demanding nature of the work was causing burnout, but their dedication and passion kept them going. Initially, they had targeted students after school, but they realized the challenge of accessibility; therefore, they switched to an in-school model, providing trained tutors that were embedded in schools all year round. To enhance financial sustainability, they diversified their revenue streams intentionally, among grants, public sources, and earned revenue from school districts. In addition, to reduce reliance on a single school district, they expanded to work with various school districts.

Tom's journey highlights the importance of dedication, salesmanship, adaptability and improvisation, grit and determination, and diversification in social entrepreneurship. It also sheds light on the complexities and evolving nature of the social entrepreneurship landscape that requires focus, agility, and open-mindedness to operate, adapt, and pivot based on what is available, whether it is resources, information, or partnerships.

Previous studies have indicated that dealing with resource limitations is typical for social entrepreneurs. These limitations are driven by factors such as lack of personal wealth, the inability or unwillingness to take on debt, or perhaps pursuing opportunities that are of little interest to funders and investors. Consequently, social entrepreneurs must look for alternative sources of revenue by using bricolage, defined as making do with what is at hand (Desa & Basu, 2013).

Davidsson, Baker, and Senyard (2017) introduced the theory of "entrepreneurial bricolage" and concluded that bricolage comes into play more heavily in the start-up phase of an enterprise but tends to subside as firms grow and scale; experienced entrepreneurs use bricolage more than new and first-time entrepreneurs; and the use of bricolage results in entrepreneurs being more flexible and adaptable in their social mission goals and business model. Bojica, Jimenez, Nava, and Fuentes-Fuentes (2018) researched the role of bricolage in the growth phase of social enterprise and showed that the impact of bricolage on the growth of an enterprise is dependent on resource availability, the entrepreneur's ability to direct the resources autonomously, and the diversity and tenure of the leadership team.

Baker, Miner, and Easley (2003) studied the process of improvisation and the issues that are associated with it in social entrepreneurship and addressed four improvisational processes: (1) strategic improvisation; (2) tactical improvisation; (3) network bricolage; and (4) improvisational competencies. Strategic and tactical improvisation results from balancing the enterprise's long-term goals with the tactical short-term priorities of the enterprise. Network bricolage results from the reliance and dependence on existing contacts and networks. Improvisational competencies are the skills of problem-solving and raising capital that social entrepreneurs develop over time as a result of their perpetual resource-poor environment. The extant literature identifies various measures that social entrepreneurs take to deal with their limited resources, including their reliance on their networks, financial bootstrapping, and effectuation strategies. These measures require resourcefulness on the part of social entrepreneurs as well as developing and nurturing strong relationships.

Starr and MacMillan's (1990) research on social resourcing and Peterson's (1995) research on social contracting emphasized that social entrepreneurs must rely on their personal networks including family, friends, and stakeholders to gain support and raise capital. Harrison et al. (2004) defined financial bootstrapping as the utilization of resources that are neither owned nor controlled by the social entrepreneur, such as owner financing, subsidized financing, resource-sharing agreements with other organizations, payment deferrals, and tight inventory management.

As highlighted earlier, Sarasvathy's (2001) strategy of effectuation is also a method that social entrepreneurs use to cope with resource constraints. Effectuation is a decision-making approach in which an entrepreneur begins with a range of possible options instead of a pre-determined and definitive goal or objective and then aims to respond and adapt intuitively by accepting and exploiting environmental uncertainties (Sarasvathy, 2004).

My group of social entrepreneurs revealed a close connection between the practice of bricolage and improvisation. In fact, the definition of improvisation as individuals "making do with materials at hand" (Miner et al., 2001, p. 333) appears quite similar to that of bricolage. Similarly, Baker et al. (2003, p. 256) noted that the concept of bricolage is "a construct frequently used to describe the resource set invoked by improvisation."

My research revealed that improvisation as a subsisting response is driven by a number of additional factors, including the parsimonious nature of social entrepreneurs, their ongoing experimentation and learning from failure, active listening and learning, and being agile, flexible, and willing to reshape and adapt the enterprise's business model as needed.

CHAPTER 11:

RALLYING – PROMOTING, EDUCATING, AND INSPIRING

All social entrepreneurs spoke of the constant rallying that was required on their part to enlist the interest and support of funders, partners, and stakeholders. They spoke of their relentless marketing, selling, and communicating efforts as being essential to gaining support and changing the mindsets of key stakeholders. The benefits of rallying included individual support in the form of coaching, mentoring, investing, and even recruiting co-founders for their enterprises, as well collective support for the co-creation of strategies and solutions to achieve a greater societal impact.

The informants emphasized that building trust and credibility with partners and stakeholders is critical to garnering their support. Accomplishing these goals requires active rallying through marketing, selling, persuasion, and negotiation on the part of social entrepreneurs. Several informants spoke of the art of persuasion in aligning the interests of the stakeholders and partners with the mission of the enterprise. One informant spoke of the need to have influential board members, who may not have deep pockets but must have connections in applicable constituents – businesses, government, foundations, communities, etc.

The deployment of social marketing also comes into play in the recruitment and retention of key talent. One informant claimed that aligning employees with the mission was more critical than their intellectual abilities, experiences, and competencies. Another informant spoke of the need to hire and develop a values-based team for a values-based organization, as they are the biggest reason for a company's success. Several informants noted that although it is critically important to sell their mission and vision to external stakeholders, it is equally important to market their social mission to potential and existing employees in order to attract and retain top talent in a resource-constrained enterprise and sector.

All social entrepreneurs also emphasized the importance of forming, building, and nurturing relationships with funders, board members, and other key stakeholders in the community. Selling the social mission and vision of the enterprise, viewing stakeholders as key relationships versus transactions, and relying on individual conversations to share their passion and enthusiasm leads to building credibility, trust, and influence with the stakeholders and in the community.

A social entrepreneur rallies and enlists support from stakeholders and leverages networks and relationships to garner support for the social enterprise. Doing so requires constant communication, advocacy, marketing, and storytelling in order to change mindsets and encourage stakeholders to become funders, investors, and supporters. Rallying enables social entrepreneurs to manage inertial, structural, and relational tensions. Throughout the four stages of social entrepreneurship, social entrepreneurs must balance stakeholder relationships.

I had the opportunity to speak with Tessie San Martin, who was President and CEO of Plan International USA at that time. Plan International USA is a girls' rights organization that helps overcome gender oppression and inequality. Tessie spoke about her journey into the nonprofit and social sector and her passion for international development since her teenage years. Early in her career, she followed a more traditional path of consulting for many years before entering the social sector on a full-time basis.

Tessie shared a formative experience from her youth when she volunteered to vaccinate children in Paraguay through an organization called Amigos de las Americas. At the onset, she lacked the knowledge and training to do this work but was able to engage, learn, and fulfill the task successfully. She attributes her early exposure to leadership and problem-solving to this experience, where she had to make in-the-moment decisions in challenging situations. She reflected on the power of youth empowerment and leadership and believes that providing such experiences to our youth can instill confidence and problem-solving skills in them as well.

She discussed the advantages and the power of working in the civil society sector that provides credibility and access to influencing government policies, especially in the field of foreign assistance and aid effectiveness. In addition to her rallying of external stakeholders, such as the government, donors, and partners to garner support and resources, she spoke of her rallying the internal stakeholders, such as the board and leadership, to gain alignment and change the operating model by introducing social enterprise concepts into a traditional nonprofit organization. She emphasized the importance of achieving measurable social impact while maintaining a sustainable financial model. This included instilling the importance of accountability, empowerment, and innovation in the organization in addressing social challenges.

Rallying is also necessary to educate, inspire, build relationships, trust, and credibility with partners and stakeholders. Previous studies in social entrepreneurship have highlighted the concept of collective entrepreneurship, meaning the power of utilizing collective action to solve social problems. Sautet (2002) emphasized the need for collective action, as the ability to solve dynamic and complex social problems is often spread across multiple actors and not found in a single individual. Previous research also discusses various approaches to dealing with the conflicts between social and financial goals, mission drift resulting from stakeholder engagement, and the divergent interests and motives of the various stakeholders. This requires persuasion, negotiations, and compromises that often underlie formal rules and structures in social entrepreneurship.

Mitznneck and Besharov (2018) identified three compromises that entrepreneurs must make when relying on numerous partners and stakeholders: temporal compromises, structural compromises, and collaborative compromises. Temporal compromises refer to frequent shifts in priorities between the social mission and financial goals. Structural compromises enable partners and stakeholders to incorporate projects of their personal choosing into the priorities of the enterprise. Collaborative compromises involve the joint development of the social mission and commercial goals.

Researchers have also investigated the role of social marketing. However, most studies have dealt with influencing changes in behavior in a specific target audience regarding certain products. Lefebver (2011) defined social marketing as the utilization of traditional marketing frameworks to develop innovative solutions to solve complex and perplexing social issues. All of my informants emphasized the need to market the social mission of the enterprise to their funders, partners, and stakeholders to gain their interest, support, alignment, and trust. Kotler and Levy (1969, p. 15) underscored the importance of marketing by saying that it is "not whether to market or not to market; for no organization can avoid marketing. The choice is whether to do it well or poorly, and on this necessity the case for organizational marketing is basically founded."

Saxton (1996) introduced five direct marketing strategies for non-profit organizations: donation-led, intimacy-led, audience-led, product-led, and multi-product. My research indicates that, of these techniques, the intimacy-led strategy, which is rooted in relationships, is the most relevant in social entrepreneurship in developing trust, long-term relationships, and mission alignment with key stakeholders. Previous research on relationship marketing has been in the context of for-profit business-to-business ventures that are designed to produce economic value. However, relationship marketing is very relevant to non-profit social exchanges and business-to-consumer marketing in which either one or both businesses may receive economic and/or social value. The rallying that my informants emphasized included the importance of developing and nurturing relationships with partners and stakeholders. Doing so led to greater trust, credibility, and alignment among the various constituents. In addition to financial support, other benefits of rallying came in the form of ongoing coaching, mentoring, advisory services, and long-term support that are essential for social entrepreneurs.

CHAPTER 12:

PERSISTING – REFUSING TO GIVE UP

Another consistent theme derived from my interview data revealed that social entrepreneurs are undyingly and unrelentingly persistent. My informants described their persistence in three forms. First, they are persistent in balancing the tensions and trade-offs, evident in their constant hustle to market and sell their vision and ideas to their stakeholders. One informant described his experience of selling to his stakeholders as repeating the same message 10,000 times, connecting social issues and specific topics that at first glance do not seem to be connected, and leading to shifting their paradigms. Several informants viewed this constant hustle as necessary in their attempt to solve problems that are worth solving, regardless of the time and effort required.

Second, their persistence was also apparent in their unwillingness to give up and in their belief that nothing is impossible. My informants shared numerous experiences that highlighted the persistence and resilience of social entrepreneurs, particularly in the face of adversity. One social entrepreneur spoke of having a dissonant attitude in knowing that you may fail the next day, but at the same time, believing that you won't, and then just forging ahead with that belief. Despite the tensions they faced throughout their social entrepreneurial life cycle, they were unphased by the amount of work required on their part. They refused to be paralyzed by the challenges they encountered but rather, learned to work around them.

Third, their relentless focus on their mission enabled them to block out and be undeterred by all the noise they faced during this social entrepreneurial journey. One informant said that to him, giving up would mean hurting himself. Therefore, believing in the mission kept him steadfast on his journey. Another informant spoke of having rock solid confidence in his idea and being undeterred by naysayers. When faced with controversy and adversity, these social entrepreneurs took risks, made personal sacrifices, and found alternate ways to sell their ideas, using their knowledge and experience as a strategic and competitive advantage. Many informants spoke of getting energy, inspiration, enthusiasm, reinforcement, and a strong sense of accountability from their mission and purpose, and from the people they served.

Finally, a social entrepreneur's unwillingness to give up leads to their resilience and persistence. Remaining focused on the social mission and having the resolve to continue to persevere in the face of ongoing challenges and roadblocks enables social entrepreneurs to balance relational and structural tensions. Social entrepreneurs require a great deal of persistence in balancing personal and social goals and commitments, operating constraints, and the dilemma they face in launching versus operating a social enterprise and in operating versus exiting a social enterprise. These factors require social entrepreneurs to modify and adapt their own expectations with regard to achieving social goals, while also meeting investor and stakeholder expectations.

I would label Gretchen Zucker as a serial social entrepreneur. She has co-founded and run social enterprises such as Her House, a women-led organization that built houses for single mothers in Washington, DC, and Youth Venture, which encourages and enables every young person to become a changemaker for the good of the world. Her latest social venture,

Fieldstone Trust LLC, which was founded in 2019, brings investment and system-level impact advising to affordable housing projects that are centered on flipping the script on landlord-tenant relations by building communities of changemakers in mobile home parks and affordable apartment communities.

Gretchen spoke of growing up in the Midwestern part of the US and developing an interest in international affairs and foreign languages during high school. In fact, her career in Africa stemmed from her study of French in high school, which led her to want to live and work in Francophone Africa. Gretchen first heard of Ashoka while working at McKinsey, where she was involved in management consulting for social entrepreneurs. As described earlier, Ashoka has played a significant role in promoting social entrepreneurship around the world and Gretchen has continued to provide consulting services to Ashoka over the past two decades. Gretchen's motivation for pursuing social impact work came from her upbringing, her experiences in community service, and her French teacher in high school. She found the idea of making a difference in people's lives to be both empowering and addictive. She also noted that Ashoka has played a significant role in her career path and her commitment to driving social change.

Gretchan believed that the scale of the Fieldstone Trust LLC initiative could help address various inequalities, including income and racial disparities, by connecting low-income tenant communities to social innovations and by empowering property managers and tenants to form "community empowerment circles" that collectively solve problems in the community and drive positive change. A portion of the financial returns in these real estate investments would fund new social innovations from Ashoka Fellows and other social entrepreneurs that could, in turn, further benefit the communities being invested in. However, she also discussed the challenges of convincing traditional investors to consider mobile home parks as an impact investment asset class and the need to bridge the gap between profit-making and social impact in the real estate sector. Despite the myriad of challenges she has faced, Gretchen highlighted the importance of building relationships, finding like-minded partners, and gradually convincing investors to embrace the concept of impact investing in this unconventional field.

In describing her experiences and insights as a social entrepreneur, Gretchen emphasized the importance of experimentation and learning and trying different approaches to solve root problems. She noted that this process of learning by trial and error and the process of changing people's mindsets to understand and embrace new ideas often takes years to materialize and underscored the maximum degree of patience, persistence, and resilience required in social entrepreneurship.

Previous studies have maintained that persistence is a necessary ingredient for commercial entrepreneurs, particularly during the start-up phase of their enterprise. Wu, Matthews, and Dagher (2007) maintained that entrepreneurs' persistent and tenacious behaviors are driven by their results orientation and need for greater achievement. Erikson (2002) attributed entrepreneurs' persistence to their optimism. Their persistence in remaining true to their mission and driving their vision forward enable them to cope with the numerous barriers and roadblocks they face in operating their ventures.

My informants validated and expanded on these studies by highlighting the persistence that social entrepreneurs must have to respond to their many tensions. It is only through their unwavering persistence, the unwillingness to give up, and the belief that nothing is impossible, that they can remain unflappable and undeterred by the barriers and tensions that they deal with on a routine basis.

CHAPTER 13:

LEVERAGING – CO-CREATING WITH COLLABORATIVE ENTREPRENEURSHIP

The information derived from my interviews with the social entrepreneurs highlighted their significant reliance on and leveraging of their networks for mission, financial, and operational support. However, it also provided insights into a few new aspects. Several informants spoke of their privileged upbringing that paved their path towards the pursuit of social entrepreneurship. They shared their experiences in childhood and adolescence and highlighted their own privileges resulting from their family, faith, education, community, network, and environment, contrasting their situation with those who lacked such privileges.

A few informants attributed this privilege to being lucky and simply being in the right place at the right time. Others attributed it to their family's wealth, their Ivy League education, or their social network of high-net-worth individuals. These factors enabled them to leverage their social capital in garnering financial support from their network of friends and family in the launch and growth phases of their social enterprise.

Several informants spoke of being privileged and feeling fortunate due to their race and gender and wanting to pay it forward. A few male informants spoke about their white man's privilege in giving them the confidence to pursue their vision, a privilege that opened doors and opportunities for them along their journey. Hence, they were able to leverage this confidence in raising support for their enterprise and helping them cope with the various tensions in launching and operating their social enterprise. Conversely, a few female and non-Caucasian social entrepreneurs I spoke with expressed anger and disappointment at having to face chauvinism and white supremacy in the American system.

Carrie Rich has been the Co-Founder and CEO of The Global Good Fund since 2011, a nonprofit social enterprise that serves social entrepreneurs, organizations, and philanthropists. The Global Good Fund's fellowship program provides coaching, mentoring, and leadership development to young leaders as being the most effective way to create positive business impact and lasting social change. She also co-founded The Global Impact Fund, a for-profit venture capital fund to invest in socially impactful businesses.

Carrie recalled that while she was employed with Inova Health Systems, she had the benefit of having Knox Singleton (former CEO of Inova Health Systems) as a mentor. On her 26th birthday, he gave her a birthday card with a $100 check inside and a note that read, "Here is the money I would have spent taking you and your colleagues to lunch for your birthday. Now you can start to live your dream." The dream Knox mentioned was an idea Carrie had presented to him a few months earlier – an idea to pair emerging young leaders with executives who have top-tier experience and a desire to help and mentor rising entrepreneurs. This led to Carrie and Knox launching The Global Good Fund. About a decade later, The Global Good Fund, through its fellowship program, had impacted the lives of more than 10 million people around the world. This is a powerful example of leveraging relationships and networks to co-create impact through collaborative entrepreneurship.

Carrie went on to discuss her journey into social entrepreneurship, noting that her interest in social good was greatly influenced by her upbringing and her parents, who were in the public health domain and emphasized giving back to society. In high school, she had the opportunity to volunteer in Jamaica, which further shaped her perspectives regarding social entrepreneurship. She pursued a degree in health administration and learned about the power of helping people through business. Carrie took an unconventional academic path and created opportunities for herself, which ultimately led to the start of The Global Good Fund. She also emphasized the role of volunteers and alumni in the organization's success, noting that making it easy for people to get involved is essential. She also spoke of the need to create a culture that attracts professionals seeking purpose and significance in their work.

Carrie highlighted the significance of Knox's mentorship and co-sponsorship in launching The Global Good Fund. She also emphasized the importance of building a supportive and diverse board of directors, acknowledging feedback, and not striving for perfection but taking action and adapting/evolving as needed. Like other social entrepreneurs, she too faced many challenges during the start-up phase, highlighting issues related to her age and gender dynamics that she handled with grace and composure, which demonstrated her leadership qualities and attracted solid supporters to The Global Good Fund.

Carrie's success story as a social entrepreneur was enabled by her privileges, including growing up in a stable and secure environment, her initiative and ability to self-design a major in college tailored to her interests, her first job through her network, and then a CEO who became a mentor, gave her opportunities to grow, learn, and think big, and later co-founded the social enterprise with her. Despite the many challenges and hardships she has faced and continues to face, her focus, commitment, and dedication to her mission enables her to persevere and be unphased by the significant amount of work and effort, as she "does not even think about it."

It is undeniable that social entrepreneurs face significant challenges from the external environment as well as from their various stakeholders. Examples include domestic and global influences, federal, state, and local government regulations, socio-economic factors, and general lifestyle shifts affecting donors, volunteers, partners, and competitors in this expanding landscape. While many social entrepreneurs have embraced and adopted a stakeholder orientation approach to address these changes, many have not, possibly due to lack of awareness, resources, and time. Social entrepreneurs must work with various stakeholders – partners, peers, donors, volunteers, and benefactors – to achieve larger social goals. A stakeholder-oriented organization can simultaneously work with and mobilize its key stakeholders to bring about social change. The organization can collaborate with partners, peers, and other community and industry constituents to satisfy the wants and needs of key external stakeholders and leverage and complement each other's strengths and weaknesses to better serve their beneficiaries and society at large. As a result, a stakeholder-oriented organization can earn and command the respect of its peers. In doing so, these organizations can improve their individual and collective effectiveness in realizing their mission. Adopting a stakeholder orientation enables a social entrepreneur to optimize the knowledge obtained from the various groups in informing its strategy and decision-making, leading to the achievement of the enterprise's social mission.

Further, leveraging privilege and luck leads them to rely on their social status and community stature to garner support, and source capital and expertise for their enterprise. Asking for help and leveraging available resources are important to ensure the long-term sustainability of a social enterprise. Doing so also requires a degree of self-awareness. Social entrepreneurs must know their own strengths, weaknesses, and limitations and know when it is time to step aside or pass the baton to others to lead the enterprise, as warranted. However, they seldom do so due to failure, which is always used as a learning opportunity. In fact, one entrepreneur described their failures as a burnt forest that regenerates and regrows beautifully.

Previous research has established that the emphasis in social entrepreneurship is on the individual entrepreneur as the lone entrepreneurial actor more than as a collective model (Austin et al., 2007; Bornstein, 2007; Dees et al., 2001; Leadbeater, 1997; Spear, 2006). However, other scholars have shown that "collective leadership," where several members play complementary roles, is critical in achieving strategic change in pluralistic organizations (Denis, Lamothe, & Langley, 2001). This concept can be extended to the broader community that is characterized by a common set of objectives. Therefore, collective leadership enables individuals, organizations, and communities with different roles and influences to unite and collaborate in solving social programs and have a social impact that extends beyond individual and organizational boundaries. Doing so requires social entrepreneurs to rely heavily on alliances and collaborations with partners, community leaders, volunteers, and other social enterprises. The notion of "competition" is replaced by "collective social entrepreneurship," where multiple individuals or groups from different sectors come together to solve a common social problem (Montgomery, Dacin, & Dacin, 2012). This intra- and cross-sector collaboration can lead to a significant social impact at the local, national, and global levels.

Therefore, the focus on social entrepreneurs as lone actors runs the risk of overlooking the vital role played by outside actors, stakeholders, networks, organizations, and institutions in overcoming barriers to success and in influencing broader public discourse. From this perspective, much of social entrepreneurship appears, in fact, to be collaborative and collective, drawing on a broad array of support, cooperation, and alliances to build awareness, obtain resources and, ultimately, make change happen.

Partnerships are also essential for social enterprises because it is through partnerships that social enterprises acquire funding, volunteers, and distribution outlets. As a result, social enterprises with partnerships are able to serve more people and have a stronger social impact. Partnerships in social enterprises also help meet strategic needs and provide social opportunities, enhance the enterprises' credibility and legitimacy, augment their dynamic capabilities, and promote organizational learning. Therefore, a social enterprise's ability to create social value depends heavily on its ability to create collaborative partnerships and alliances.

Ferraro, Etzion, and Gehman (2015) provided a construct of collective entrepreneurship used by corporations and described it as building a participatory structure in which a diverse set of stakeholders are brought together to tackle a social mission and work collectively on developing and implementing solutions to address the problem. They defined multivocal inscription as a set of actions undertaken to achieve stakeholder alignment and coordination around the social mission and maintained that distributed experimentation involves breaking down the social mission's goals into small milestones as a means to promote experimentation, learning, and evolutionary progress towards the achievement of the social mission.

We have reviewed that there are many challenges that result from social entrepreneurs' reliance on the various partners and stakeholders needed to develop a collective social entrepreneurship framework for maximum social impact, and leveraging their privileges is an important subsisting response to coping with these challenges and tensions. In fact, Wernick (2021) studied the impact of people's influence and privilege on their ability to coalesce and organize groups of individuals in their networks, to align and work together to enable change and to help solve social problems in society, and maintained that by leveraging privilege, an entrepreneur can bring together wealthy individuals to support social change.

The ability to leverage relationships effectively requires that entrepreneurs have strong social skills, defined as a set of competencies that enable individuals to interact effectively with other individuals or groups of individuals, enable them to leverage their network of family, friends, and colleagues to reach a broader base of investors and partners. The resulting benefits from these networks can come in the form of financial and non-financial resources, more information and knowledge, and enhanced reputation, trust, and cooperation from others. Collectively, these resources are often referred to as social capital, which is defined as the ability of an entrepreneur to obtain resources through social relationships. It plays an important role in helping entrepreneurs overcome the barriers and challenges in the launch and operation of new enterprises.

Recent research on network theory has highlighted the various types of networks entrepreneurs use in their drive to achieve their mission's objectives (Lechner et al., 2006). It is widely acknowledged that entrepreneurs are generally resource-starved in the launch and growth phases of their enterprise and must rely on their personal social networks to raise capital. This reliance is critically important in the launch phase of their enterprise. All social entrepreneurs I spoke with emphasized this point repeatedly and underscored their strong reliance on leveraging their family, friends, and professional networks for financial and moral support.

CHAPTER 14:

ADAPTING – CHANGING AND EVOLVING CONTINUOUSLY

My informants recounted numerous experiences that demonstrated flexibility and adaptability in their navigation through the social entrepreneurial phases. They spoke of many experiences that highlighted adaptation as an important coping mechanism for social entrepreneurs in dealing with others' narrow thinking and their unwillingness to keep an open mind. To overcome these obstacles, they had to adopt marketing and communication strategies focused on selling and reinforcing the mission. They also realized that the enterprise's social mission, program, and operating model would need to evolve to adapt to the needs of the key stakeholders and funders. Embracing and growing from the ongoing learning and then applying the learning to adjust, adapt, and evolve the social mission are essential elements of launching and operating a social enterprise.

Adapting often leads to social entrepreneurs making difficult and selective choices. Examples include choosing to engage with the right partners and investors, who are trusted, committed, supportive, and collaborative; choosing the right staff for the enterprise, who are passionate about the mission and have a service orientation; and choosing when to adapt, evolve, take risks, or even shut down the enterprise or a given program, when necessary. Several social entrepreneurs noted that to ensure alignment with and among stakeholders, they had to be selective in choosing partners and employees and had to modify and adapt their own expectations and operating models. Flexibility and adaptability are necessary subsisting responses for the social entrepreneurs' personal financial security as well as institutional survival.

Scott Beale co-founded Atlas Corps in 2006, was its CEO till 2021, and currently remains a board director. Atlas Corps is an international nonprofit organization that develops and empowers social change leaders, strengthens social organizations, and promotes innovation in the nonprofit sector around the globe. Scott shared that he grew up in Delaware, where both of his parents were teachers. His background has always been about engagement, activism, and empowering others to make social change. His early experiences were in politics, including working for the Governor of Delaware, Senator Joe Biden, and in the White House during President Bill Clinton's tenure. After working in the White House, Scott joined Ashoka's Youth Venture, and later the US Foreign Service, working at the US Embassy in India.

During his early career, Scott started two nonprofits, the 2100 Fund, focused on charitable fundraising, and Millennial Politics, aimed at creating a millennial manifesto. Both nonprofit organizations were driven by his belief in the potential of young people to create change. He eventually left the State Department and founded Atlas Corps, a nonprofit organization focused on international exchange programs. Scott's entry into the social sector, which began with his involvement in politics, viewing it as a form of service to create change, was inspired by his belief in people's potential for change, the importance of empowering individuals to make a difference, and the value of diversity of thought.

Like all other social entrepreneurs, Scott too spoke of the many challenges he faced in launching and operating Atlas Corps and his reliance on his personal and professional networks in making Atlas Corps the product of a collective endeavor, by involving people who share the idea of creating a global network of social impact leaders. Throughout our interview, Scott emphasized the importance of listening, seeking advice, and adaptability. He spoke of the general undervaluation of the social sector and the need for stronger financial planning and support. Having learned these lessons during the launch phase, including the realization that funders are often focused on specific causes rather than leadership development, he began to emphasize his organization's value proposition when seeking funding.

Scott also noted having to make a shift in Atlas Corps' funding model in response to the 2008 financial crisis, emphasizing the value of the fellows they provide to host organizations, as well as adapting to the impact of the COVID pandemic on their operations, by quickly introducing virtual programs to navigate difficult times. He adopted an approach to involve fellows in the decision-making process and created an alumni community, further illustrating the importance of stakeholder and community engagement in social entrepreneurship. Scott emphasized the importance of continuous networking, seeking advice from other social entrepreneurs, attending conferences, and learning from his own and others' experiences as a means to continuously adapting and evolving the organization as needed.

As highlighted by Scott and many other informants, social entrepreneurs must be willing to adapt their mission, goals, and operating models to achieve greater alignment with partners and stakeholders. Extant literature shows that social entrepreneurs face ongoing challenges due to the mere fact that they operate in the social sector and therefore do not have access to the financial and market support that is available in the commercial sector. Consequently, social entrepreneurs must be resourceful and persuasive in acquiring and utilizing financial, human, and political resources. They must also be persistent, flexible, and creative in identifying and solving social issues.

Baron and Markman (2000) defined social adaptability as the ability to comfortably interact with diverse individuals and to adjust and adapt to a wide range of social situations. Social entrepreneurs can be described as perfect examples of flexibility and adaptation, given their ability to adapt and evolve their strategies quickly, work on multiple initiatives simultaneously, and advance their mission through with innovation and creativity. My informants used this skill to cope with the various tensions they faced during the start-up and growth phases of their social enterprise.

Extant literature also identifies integration and separation as two ways in which social entrepreneurs respond to tensions (Smith et al., 2013). Integration refers to strategies that lead to solutions that address the tensions emanating from market and social or environmental forces, and separation strategies lead to the separation and breakdown of goals into milestones or focus areas. Temporal strategies lead to vacillating between the enterprise's social mission and financial goals as needed (Jay, 2013). My informants revealed that these contradictory mission-market tensions are ongoing and routine in social entrepreneurship and the best way to deal with these tensions is by embracing new ideas and being open to adapting and evolving as needed.

Adaptation is a subsisting response that is centered on listening, learning, flexibility, and agility to deal with conflicting tensions and priorities in launching and operating a social enterprise. While social entrepreneurs deploy various coping mechanisms to manage, mitigate, or overcome the tensions they face throughout their journey, my informants also revealed that these tensions are typical of the social sector. Therefore, they often accept and live with these tensions and contradictions rather than exert energy or invest resources to resolve them. In other words, tensions are assumed to be a part of the business and therefore are accepted and worked around to avoid the risks of potential mission drift. Siegner, Pinkse, and Panwar (2018) described these unaddressed tensions as leading to social mission disjunction because social entrepreneurs may choose to deliver benefits to some beneficiaries or targeted geographies, while ignoring other beneficiaries and geographies. As a result, they provide only a partial or limited solution to the social problems they seek to address. Therefore, social entrepreneurs are constantly juggling conflicting priorities, making decisions, and adapting to approaches that lead to constant change and evolution, as driven by various external and internal forces.

In reviewing the tensions faced by social entrepreneurs and the coping mechanisms they often deploy to balance, manage, mitigate, and subsist in responding to the tensions, there isn't a one-to-one co-relation between the tensions and responses. Figure 6 shows the loosely intertwined relationship between the balancing tensions that require the various subsisting responses.

***Figure* 6.** Balancing Tensions Require Subsisting Responses

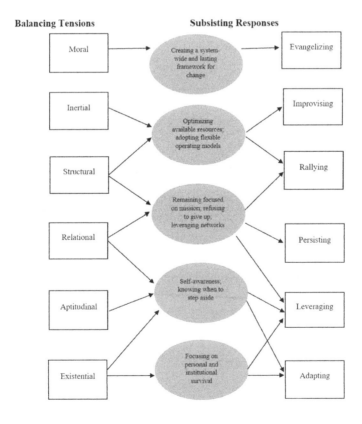

CHAPTER 15:

SOCIAL ENTREPRENEURIAL ATTRIBUTES

On the surface, the fundamental business model of a social enterprise may appear like a commercial enterprise. Nevertheless, launching and operating a social enterprise in a capitalist economy continues to be extremely challenging. The term "social entrepreneurship" is often used to describe the role of a risk-taking individual to create social change. Therefore, it is important to examine the leadership characteristics of a social entrepreneur, as well as the origin of these traits, in understanding the intentions and motivations that lead to an individual becoming a social entrepreneur.

Big Five Personality Traits

The personality traits of leaders and entrepreneurs have been studied extensively. The Big Five leadership characteristics (also referred to as OCEAN) – Openness, Conscientiousness, Extraversion, Agreeableness, and Neuroticism — is a popular and widely studied model in the context of traditional entrepreneurship. Studies of the Big Five personality traits model suggest that entrepreneurship results more from openness, conscientiousness, and extraversion and less from agreeableness and neuroticism. Koe Hwee Nga (2010) noted that the Big Five personality characteristics have an impact on social entrepreneurship intentions and added that these traits as well as other key traits, such as innovation, social networks, sustainability, and financial returns, should be incorporated into the business education curriculum.

Entrepreneurial intention serves as the aspiration to launch a business and can be defined as something "to do, to be, or to have" and as a process or a conscious willingness in the present to create or realize an experience or result in the future. In this context, Lopez-Nunez, Rubio-Valdehita, Aparicio-Garcia, and Diaz-Ramiro (2020) discussed the "psychological profile" of an entrepreneur and the role of the Big Five personality traits in entrepreneurial intentions and entrepreneurial behavior. They added other traits such as ambiguity, tolerance, emotional intelligence, and problem-solving as essential for entrepreneurs. However, these studies focused on traditional entrepreneurs and did not address the personality traits of social entrepreneurs, including the factors that influence social entrepreneurs' intentions, motivations, and behaviors.

Although some leadership characteristics may appear to be similar for a social and entrepreneurs, it is the social entrepreneurs' service-oriented leadership attributes that makes them stronger collaborators and more able to adapt to changing demands. Their ability to bridge diverse stakeholders and adapt to the changing environment over the long term go beyond the Big Five leadership characteristics.

Servant Leadership

The seed for a social enterprise is often sown by a social entrepreneur who is committed to solving a social problem or problems in society. The term "servant leadership" was coined by retired AT&T executive Robert Greenleaf (1977/2002, p. 27) in his 1970 essay, "The Servant as a Leader" and has since become a leadership paradigm for organizations. The key characteristics of a servant leader are listening, empathy, healing, awareness, persuasion, conceptualization, foresight, commitment, and building community. Petrovskaya and Mirakyan (2018) established a conceptual link between the research domains of social entrepreneurship and servant leadership by exploring the notion that social entrepreneurs may have specific leadership attributes that would classify them as servant leaders. This research identified all of the key servant leadership attributes found in social entrepreneurs, and added the attributes of altruism, humility, integrity, trust in others, and empathy.

Servant leadership has also been studied as a multidimensional construct (Ehrhart, 2004; Liden et al., 2014; van Dierendonck & Nuijten, 2011). These dimensions include: (1) emotional healing, which involves the degree to which the leader cares about others' well-being; (2) creating value for the community, which captures the leader's passion to help the community and encourage others to be active in it; (3) conceptual skills, reflecting the leader's problem-solving acumen in addressing complex social issues; (4) empowering, assessing the degree to which the leader entrusts others with responsibility, autonomy, and decision-making influence; (5) helping subordinates grow and succeed, which captures the extent to which the leader helps others reach their full potential; (6) putting subordinates first, assessing the degree to which the leader prioritizes the needs of others before tending to his/her own needs; and (7) behaving ethically, which includes being honest, trustworthy, and serving as a model of integrity.

We have already established that leadership is a critical factor that determines the success of social enterprises. Servant leadership is a leadership style that focuses on the development of followers and stresses to them the importance of serving others. Social exchange theory (Blau, 1964) has been used to explain why servant leadership enhances organizational commitment. More specifically, key servant leadership behaviors, such as forming strong relationships with followers and helping them develop and succeed, leads to increased emotional attachment with the leader and the enterprise. Empirical research provides support for such assertions.

For example, Miao et al. (2014) found a strong relationship between servant leadership and the affective commitment of civil servants in China. Similarly, Liden et al. (2008) established a strong relationship between servant leadership and the organizational commitment of employees in a commercial organization in the US.

This relationship between servant leadership and organizational commitment is even stronger in social enterprises, given it is a style of leadership that fits with the mission of social enterprises to create value for the greater good. Servant leaders guide followers to emulate their behavior by prioritizing the needs of others above their own. This serving culture directly influences engagement, productivity, and job satisfaction. Given its focus on leader behaviors that help followers realize their full potential, servant leadership represents a positive approach to organizational behavior, meaning the strength and capacity of such positive leaders can be developed, managed, and measured to enable the improvement of organizational performance. Smith, Organ, and Near (1983) developed the term "organizational citizenship behavior" (OCB) as being an employee behavior that is above and beyond the call of duty and is therefore discretionary and not rewarded in the context of an organization's formal reward structure. OCB has direct applicability to social entrepreneurship, as evidenced in all of my conversations with social entrepreneurs.

Metapreneur

Lessem (1986) introduced the concept of a "metapreneur" as an evolved leader who combines the traits of "Doing, Thinking, and Feeling" that are determined by underlying motive and developed by versatility. Lessem described the transition of the entrepreneur in the 19th century, to the manager in the 20th century, and to the metapreneur in the 21st century. He defined metapreneurs as transformed managers and categorized them into seven groups: doers, feelers, thinkers, those with willpower, organizers, intuiters, and creators. Lessem also provided seven basic training-oriented paths to achieving metrapreneurial level management skills. However, this study was limited to the commercial sector and did not include self-awareness, morality, consciousness, emotional intelligence, empathy, creativity, and other traits that drive people's sense of moral obligation to society and humanity at large.

Social Identity Theory

Social identity theory (Tajfel, 1972; Tajfel & Turner, 1979) can help improve our understanding of social entrepreneurs by establishing that social entrepreneurial activities are an expression of a social entrepreneur's individual identity. For example, social entrepreneurial activities are an expression of a servant leader's individual identity or of themselves. In examining questions such as, "Who am I?" and "What is my role in society?", Plato, Aristotle, and other ancient Greek philosophers shed light on the concept of the self and the origins of an individual's concept of self.

Social identity theory, which originated in psychology, deals with identity as it relates to an individual's social relationship and to his or her membership in groups or social categories (such as a social class, family unit, a group sharing a common interest, or a member of a community). There are three elements of social identity theory: (1) interaction with others, signifying the emotional value of group membership, engagement, and collaboration; (2) level of inclusiveness, emphasizing the inclination to act as a member of a social group; and (3) engagement in behaviors and actions for the greater good, that is, working on solving a common social problem.

These elements of social identity theory are also key to understanding the motivations and construct of servant leadership. Their missionary identity (Tajfel & Turner, 1979) makes a servant leader a powerful agent of change in creating and convening platforms to advance causes that are generally social or environmental in nature. Initial studies of social identity theory in the fields of psychology and sociology have given rise to a possible intersection point between social identity theory and identity theory. Davis et al. (2019) explored collective identity as a group's social identity that emerges from activities centered on social activism. Their study included the influence of an individual's identity and the social environment in the development of a collective identity but did not investigate the effects of such programs and theories on the creation of social entrepreneurs or their ability to manage and mitigate conflicts and competing priorities in achieving their enterprise's social mission. Similarly, Stets and Burke (2000) explored identity theory and social identity theory in developing a general theory of the self that is driven by the "group, role, and person." Pan (2019) connected personal identity (related to individual behavior), social identity (related to social behavior), and role identity (related to an individual's role-based behavior) to understanding the social entrepreneurship construct. He noted that social entrepreneurs' actions are largely driven by their personal identity.

To expand on previous research, I found it helpful to study whether certain unique social entrepreneurial attributes are required or contribute to enabling the subsisting responses and coping mechanisms from social entrepreneurs. This approach revealed a typology of unique attributes that social entrepreneurs possess that help them survive and thrive in the perpetually challenging environment of social entrepreneurship. As Figure 7 illustrates, I categorized these characteristics into six attributes – crusader, bricoleur, proselytizer, sedulousness, opportunist, and conscious dreamer.

Figure 7. Social Entrepreneurial Attributes

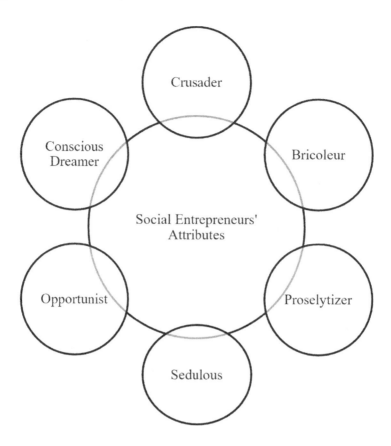

Entrepreneurial Behavior

Jebarajakirthy and Thaichon (2015) developed a conceptual framework for understanding and developing entrepreneurial behavior, although it was limited to considering its implications for social marketers. Entrepreneurial behavior has been defined as

... a process of strategic thinking required to maintain an independent belief system that supports discovery, exploration and exploitation of wealth opportunities that destabilize prior market equilibrium, demonstrating innovation, creativity and entrepreneurism to generate new flexible, adaptive and responsible market spaces that reward people ready, able and willing to meet emerging individual and societal needs, wants, hopes and expectations. (Benjamin, 2006, p. 6)

In more recent studies, the theory of planned behavior (Ajzen, 1991), initially originating in social psychology, has become a popular framework for understanding intentions and entrepreneurial behavior. Broadly speaking, intention is defined as an individual's inclination and willingness to perform a given action. However, in the context of entrepreneurship, intention has been defined as "a self-acknowledged conviction by a person that they intend to set up a new business venture and consciously plan to do so at some point in the future" (Thompson, 2009, p. 676). The theory of planned behavior provides three antecedents to intentions: attitudes (favorable or unfavorable); subjective norms (social pressure); and perceived behavioral control (the effort of engaging in the behavior). The theory of planned behavior is often used to explain the launch and growth of a business as a planned behavior. Krueger et al. (2000, p. 414) noted that entrepreneurship is a deliberate process and that in fact, "much of human behavior is planned." However, although the theory of planned behavior has proven to be a predictor of entrepreneurial intentions and the stages of change theory indicates how behavior changes over time, it fails to address the development aspect of entrepreneurial behavior.

In examining the traits and attributes of social entrepreneurs, it is helpful to study the factors that lead individuals to become social entrepreneurs. Cohen and Katz (2016) studied the integration between psychoanalytical and existential psychological theories in examining why people become social entrepreneurs. They described this process as occurring in different spheres and shaping the life study of a social entrepreneur. They detailed these spheres as the personality sphere; the family sphere, including family dynamics and significant experiences in childhood; the social sphere, including formative events occurring outside the family; and the moral sphere, which includes ideologies and attitudes.

There are existing theories such as the personality-trait theory to help better understand the factors that lead to the emergence of social entrepreneurs. Such personality traits are developed by innate nurturing, socialization, and education and drive entrepreneurial decision-making. However, personality traits are somewhat static and do not consider other factors such as education and political environment, which can also play a role in the emergence of social entrepreneurs.

Motivation is also an area of study in entrepreneurship and has been defined as a psychological process that governs, fuels, and sustains action. Renko (2012) posited that the motivations of nascent entrepreneurs are often driven by the desire to bring about social change, rather than personal or shareholder wealth creation. Baston (2008) and Grant (2007) introduced the term "prosocial motivation" as encapsulating a social entrepreneur's motivation to help other people, which is driven by a genuine concern for them. Yitshaki and Kropp (2016) studied the motivation patterns of social entrepreneurs through a life study analysis. They demonstrated that most social entrepreneurs were motivated by "pull factors" based on past or current life experiences, whereas others were motivated by "push factors," including dissatisfaction with their jobs and the desire to give back to society.

Blaga (2018) identified three sets of motivations for pursuing social entrepreneurship: intrinsic motivations (intangible rewards, such as recognition), extrinsic motivations (material rewards, such as compensation), and complex motivations (benefits and perks, such as working from home and a flexible schedule). Intrinsic motivations can be defined as doing an activity for its inherent satisfaction and extrinsic motivations as a behavior that has been influenced by an external force.

To delve further into the motivations of social entrepreneurs, it is helpful to draw on the Universal Human Values framework developed by Schwartz (1994). This theory involves 40 basic values: universalism, benevolence, tradition, conformity, security, power, achievement, hedonism, stimulation, and self-direction. This body of literature shows that social entrepreneurs are largely driven by the "self-transcendent" values of universalism and benevolence that push them beyond their own self-interests to seek the betterment of others.

Tiwari, Bhat, and Tikoria (2017) introduced emotional intelligence and creativity as factors that influence the formation of social entrepreneurial intentions. Emotional intelligence is defined as the aptitude and ability of individuals to manage and direct his/her emotions and feelings sensibly. Two models have been developed to understand emotional intelligence. The mental ability model refers to people's ability to control their emotions and the mixed model or the multiple intelligence theory (Gardner, 2004) refers to the various personal attributes such as achievement and flexibility needed to manage one's emotions and relationships.

Mair and Noboa (2006) developed a model of social entrepreneurship intentions using specific variables and concluded that the intention to start a social enterprise develops from perceived desirability, which is influenced by cognitive emotional factors of empathy and moral judgment, and perceived feasibility, which is influenced by self-efficacy and social support as enablers. Research on the unique personality traits of a social entrepreneur is still evolving and there are few existing studies about how these personality traits may influence social entrepreneur behaviors and actions.

Social Entrepreneurial Propensity

Prior to examining the unique characteristics of a social entrepreneur, I also studied the various factors that might increase the propensity or inclination of an individual to develop social entrepreneurial traits. Several scholars have examined the role of education in entrepreneurship. Thompson and Kwong (2016) argued that a mandatory school-based education can lead to successful careers in entrepreneurship by using the mere creation of a new venture as the sole measure of success. In a study focusing on the relationship between education and entrepreneurship among ethnic groups, Thompson, Jones-Evans, and Kwong (2010) highlighted the difference as being driven by the nature of the entrepreneurship education as necessity-driven versus opportunity-driven. Unfortunately, their research did not explore education related to social entrepreneurship or its impact on the creation of social entrepreneurs.

Further, Oana and Shahrazad (2016) examined the role and moral obligation of universities in the production of graduates who are civically aware, socially responsible, and have entrepreneurial attributes, as well as the moral obligation of universities to foster, enable, and create social entrepreneurs.

Several scholars have used social identity theory, maintaining that social entrepreneurial activities are an expression of a social entrepreneur's individual identity. Previous studies of this theory in the fields of psychology and sociology have given rise to a possible intersection point between social identity theory and identity theory. Davis et al. (2019) defined collective identity as a group's social identity formed through collective activism. Their study includes the influence of an individual's identity and the social environment in the development of collective identity.

Similarly, Stets and Burke (2000) used identity theory and social identity theory in developing a general theory of the self as driven by the "group, role, and person." Pan (2019) made the connection between personal identity (related to individual behavior), social identity (related to social behavior), and role identity (related to an individual's role-based behavior) to understand the social entrepreneurship construct.

Pan noted that social entrepreneurs' actions are largely driven by their personal identity.

Previous scholars have also studied the role of civil society in giving rise to social entrepreneurs and demonstrated a cause-and-effect relationship between the characteristics of civil society and those of social entrepreneurs. Oana and Shahrazad (2013) posited that civil society, which is constantly evolving and addresses the needs of society, does, in fact, foster social entrepreneurs. Chan, Ou, and Reynolds (2014) established that civic engagement in youth and adolescence plays a significant role in developing civic and social awareness in adulthood. They noted specifically the favorable impact of adolescent civic engagement on the social and emotional development of individuals, particularly among an inner-city minority cohort.

Nicholls (2011) noted that social entrepreneurs are a new generation of civic-minded individuals who are motivated to solve systemic problems around the globe. A social entrepreneur's deep sense of social awareness and moral obligation to society can be shaped through education; societal events calling for social justice; specific civic engagement activities; a personal event or experience; other factors or perhaps a combination of these factors.

Social Entrepreneurial Attributes

Most of the studies on the personality traits of social entrepreneurs differentiate the "prosocial personality" of a social entrepreneur from traditional commercial entrepreneurs. Penner and Finkelstein (1998, p. 526) defined a prosocial personality as "an enduring tendency to think about the welfare and rights of other people, to feel concern and empathy for them, and to act in a way that benefits them." My informants revealed a prosocial personality in their strong degree of empathy, which Coplan (2011, p. 40) defined as "a complex, imaginative process through which an observer simulates another person's situated psychological states while maintaining clear self-other differentiation." In other words, empathy is the understanding and sharing of the emotional state of others.

My interviewees revealed the impact of personality traits on the intentions of a social entrepreneur to launch a social enterprise. These personality traits are often developed due to the unique knowledge, values, beliefs, perceptions, and personal experiences of individuals (Kor et al., 2007). Zahra, Gedajlovic, Neubaum, and Shulman (2009) expanded on the notion of personality traits to define three types of social entrepreneurs: (1) social bricoleurs, who solve problems with available resources using creativity and innovation; (2) social constructionists, who introduce societal change through the development of new models to create and distribute wealth; and (3) social engineers, who pioneer revolutionary change and disrupt the equilibrium.

Leadership skills also come into play in addressing the conflicting dual focus of social welfare and financial sustainability for social entrepreneurs and enterprises. As discussed earlier, these dual goals give rise to tensions and contradictions for social entrepreneurs. Paradox theory offers insights into these tensions and contradictions and how to manage, mitigate, and overcome the resulting challenges (Smith & Lewis, 2011). In these situations, social entrepreneurs can either embrace and accept the tensions and attempt to address them in tandem or avoid rather than confront them.

Previous research on paradox theory suggests that there are three meta-skills that social entrepreneurs use to deal with these conflicts: acceptance, differentiation, and integration. Acceptance leads to embracing conflicts and learning to live with them. Differentiation leads to a deeper understanding of each alternative and responding accordingly. Integration leads to a synergistic approach to dealing with both alternatives simultaneously. All three skills are essential for dealing with and effectively managing the social and commercial pressures that social entrepreneurs face. They may shift their paradigm from an "either/or" approach to a "both/and" approach (Smith & Lewis, 2011), enabling them to think creatively about solving both competing needs. Miller and Sardais (2013) described an entrepreneur's ability to be optimistic and realistic, as well as persistent and adaptive, as intrinsic qualities of an entrepreneur.

It is their ability to navigate through and maneuver between social and financial goals that enables social entrepreneurs to create blended social and financial value for their enterprise and society. Previous studies have attributed the success of social entrepreneurs to their passion that evokes trust from funders, partners, and employees, and describe them as very capable people who often embody the conflicting traits of ethical fiber and a results orientation or vision and pragmatism in launching and operating their enterprises.

My research indicated the existence of several additional unique attributes in social entrepreneurs that extend beyond the personality traits of traditional entrepreneurs. On its surface, the concept of a "metapreneur" appears to be fitting to describe social entrepreneurs, who combine thought, feeling, and action in particular contexts and are "the sum of our individuality, the true spirit of our personal and corporate beings" (Lessem, 1986, p. 6). Unfortunately, Lessem's study is limited to traditional entrepreneurs and does not address the personality traits and attributes of social entrepreneurs. My research and grounded theory highlighted six key attributes that are unique to social entrepreneurs – crusader, bricoleur, proselytizer, sedulous, opportunist, and conscious dreamer. The following chapters elaborate on each of these attributes.

CHAPTER 16:

CRUSADER – SOCIAL REFORM CHAMPION

All informants exhibited a strong bent not only towards solving a specific social issue or set of societal issues but also towards creating lasting change on a global scale by developing a framework for social change. Bill Drayton is an excellent exemplar of a social crusader or reformer. He emphasized to me the importance of gaining a deeper understanding of the whole entrepreneur and greatly appreciated my research approach to examining social entrepreneurs in our everything-changing and everything-connected world.

Throughout the interview, Bill seemed to project the complete embodiment of social entrepreneurship, so much so that he was unable to separate himself from Ashoka, his social enterprise. Bill defined "social entrepreneurship" as providing three different types of change – direct service (e.g., the teacher in the classroom); systems change (i.e., a new way of organizing and growing up); and framework or mindset change (i.e., getting everyone to understand the new reality and therefore, all that is required in an 'everything-changing' and 'everything-connected' world). In his view, social entrepreneurs do not choose easy ways to make the prototype work and do not seek idiosyncratic solutions. Instead, they seek solutions that will work everywhere as they seek systems and mindset change and therefore do not get distracted easily. Bill believes that a social entrepreneur is committed to the good of all without exceptions, and therefore it doesn't even cross their mind to think about a partial set of beneficiaries. Therefore, one of the fundamental differences between social enterprise and social entrepreneurship is that social entrepreneurs run businesses that are focused on a specific social challenge, whereas social entrepreneurship is in the interests of serving all. It is not meant to benefit an individual, or group of individuals, or a specific ideology. It is focused on understanding and changing mindsets about new realities, reorganizing existing beliefs and constructs, and redefining success. And to Bill, that is a completely fundamental dividing line.

Having been an entrepreneur for six decades, Bill spoke about having a strong sense of purpose to serve all of society – local, national, and global. To do so, he said the entrepreneur must dream big, teach, and enable others, invite others, and scale the enterprise for ongoing and lasting change. Overall, his calmness, quiet resolve, and clarity of purpose demonstrated the evolution of his journey as a social entrepreneur. I was struck by how he viewed challenges as being somewhat inconsequential. Instead, he kept coming back to his idealistic laser focus on creating lasting change in the world by changing the framework and encouraging and enabling entrepreneurs to become changemakers. Bill, through the work of Ashoka, is intent on ensuring that 'everyone' has the power to be a giver, which requires 'everyone' to be a changemaker, reinforcing his belief that the ultimate human right is "the right to give".

Another social entrepreneur, Dhananjaya Kumar spoke with great passion about serving society as being his role in life and the purpose for his being. He spoke with great humility about having grown up in a village and his early education from nature and farming. His deep sense of moral obligation was rooted in his humble and modest beginnings and in observing the major sacrifices made by his parents. His interest in education as a means of helping everyone achieve peace and harmony on this planet developed quite early in his life. He spoke about the social venture that he launched four decades ago and that still exists today. He also spoke about a recent social venture focused on education reform that he is struggling to get off the ground due to limited financial resources; however, he is not deterred by that and is using other creative means to implement his programs, both virtually and physically in dozens of schools in India.

Dhananjaya spoke of facing many challenges throughout his journey, but his commitment and resolve seemed to minimize the challenges, as he found ways to work around them. When asked whether he had ever thought of exiting social entrepreneurship, he paused for a moment and responded that the thought of giving up had never even occurred to him, as giving up would mean hurting himself. He understands that making holistic changes in the education system requires change in policy, thinking, and mindsets. However, he believes in creating lasting change and continues to dedicate his life to educational reform, realizing that he is making incremental improvements that may be mere drops in the bucket but represent concrete steps in the right direction.

Rajiv Malhotra, Founder and CEO of Infinity Foundation, stated that his deep feelings of connectedness with science and spirituality were in part the result of his spiritual upbringing. Though he spoke of his lifelong interest in doing something for society and becoming a better person, he was obligated to first provide financial stability for himself and his family. Therefore, he set a personal goal to defer social entrepreneurship until he became financially secure. He maintained this commitment, and some 20 years later, in 1994, he sold his technology companies to launch a social enterprise to focus on compassion and wisdom as his two primary values to do something big and lasting for a higher cause for humanity. Rajiv is also a renowned author on topics including civilizations, cross-cultural ideologies, religion, and science.

Rajiv spoke of being viewed as a renegade and disrupter and shared his frustrations in dealing with people chasing wealth, and sadness at being disowned by and disassociated from his own family and close friends due to his controversial views and directness in dealing with naysayers and detractors. He spoke with conviction about his personal journey as a crusade of sorts and expressed appreciation for having generated interest and support from volunteers and supporters from across the world.

These and other informants displayed attributes that I likened to that of a crusader, a true advocate and champion for change, seeking societal advancement for the future sustainability of our planet. Previous research addressed the notion of collective social entrepreneurship that all of my informants also highlighted as a means of creating a durable and sustainable change. Montgomery, Dacin, and Dacin (2012) defined collective social entrepreneurship as collective and collaborative actions taken by multiple individuals to address and resolve social issues, create new frameworks and institutions, and deconstruct existing models and processes. Benford and Snow (2000, p. 614) defined collective action as "action-oriented sets of beliefs and meanings that inspire and legitimate the activities and campaigns of a social movement organization." Collective social entrepreneurs engage in three primary activities: framing, convening, and multivocality. The framing process describes the collective identification, analysis, and interpretation of social problems to bring about a call to action to enable change. Conveners are champions of change who assemble and facilitate the development and execution of solutions within and across organizational boundaries. Multivocality is the ability to mobilize and align a diverse group of stakeholders and audiences through active listening and effective communication, thereby making appeals to numerous audiences simultaneously.

My informants spoke of their lifelong quest in pursuit of their social mission, advocating for reform, and living their life with this singular focus. They felt a strong sense of connectedness with humanity and their social mission, such that they were unable to separate themselves from their mission and enterprise. They dedicated their lives to bringing about lasting social change and would not stop at anything in making continual progress towards that goal. Therefore, being a crusader and a social reform champion is a unique attribute of social entrepreneurs.

CHAPTER 17:
BRICOLEUR – RESOURCEFUL PROBLEM-SOLVER

As noted earlier, the term "bricolage" can be traced back to Claude Lévi-Strauss (1966), a cultural anthropologist who referred to a "bricoleur" as "a jack-of-all trades" who manages with the resources available. Lévi-Strauss did not provide a specific definition of bricolage but noted its characteristics, including a "bias towards action" and an acceptance of "ambiguity and messiness" that often leads to "brilliant unforeseen results." The lack of a specific definition prompted scholars from various disciplines to investigate and interpret the term.

Baker and Nelson (2005) defined bricolage as coping with the resources available and applying those resources to solve existing and new social problems. Such perpetually resource-constrained firms that are run by founders are the most common forms of business around the globe. This is even more prevalent in social entrepreneurship, which is often constrained by financial and human capital.

Di Dominico (2010) defined bricolage as an entrepreneur's reaction to resource scarcity and social bricolage as the social entrepreneur's ability to obtain resources in resource-constrained environments. Social entrepreneurs use various approaches to access resources such as social funding, financial bootstrapping, effectuation, and bricolage. Other studies have posited that social entrepreneurs do not actively seek business loans and equity financing, but rather reuse available capital to improvise and survive.

Bojica, Jimenez, Nava, and Fuentes-Fuentes (2018) studied the relationship between bricolage and the growth of a social enterprise, noting that some social entrepreneurial organizations engage in bricolage, not because they lack access to capital, but to drive organizational innovation. Their study of bricolage for growth versus bricolage out of necessity showed that the impact of bricolage on a social enterprise's growth is contingent on three factors: the availability of resources; the degree of autonomy over the available resources; and the diversity of the top management team in the organization. They emphasized the relevance of the top management team's characteristics to the role played by bricolage in the organization's growth, about the types of resources, and their re-combination, re-creation, and allocation. Therefore, bricolage can often lead to more innovation due to the bias for action in a resource-constrained environment leading to either making do, using existing resources, or recombining existing resources.

Several scholars have highlighted bricolage as a fundamental aspect of social entrepreneurship, primarily as a behavior necessary to deal with the limited financial resources in the social sector. My research has shown that bricolage is acquired through self-taught skills and experience and developed through trial and error with existing networks. The various roles the informants noted that they have played are examples of their experiences as bricoleurs. While bricolage is an important trait of social entrepreneurs, it is not sufficient in helping them manage and overcome resource constraints during the start-up and operational stages of their social enterprise.

Scott Rechler has been the Co-Director and CEO of LearnServe International since 2010. LearnServe International encourages and equips middle and high school students with diverse backgrounds with the entrepreneurial vision, confidence, tenacity, and leadership skills needed to tackle social challenges both nationally and overseas. Having grown up in Washington, DC, in a family with a strong social justice ethos, Scott spoke fondly of his family for supporting him during his early years and his spouse for being patient with him and being a co-provider for the family as he co-launched a scrappy social enterprise. However, in a decade, he has been able to grow the organization to become an enterprise that is making an impact around the world. Scott's interest in social entrepreneurship developed during his undergraduate years at Harvard, where he majored in social anthropology. His undergraduate thesis was on social entrepreneurship in Latin America. Upon returning to DC, Scott initiated a program called Bridging Boundaries DC that aimed at connecting students from various backgrounds and helping them start their social venture projects. This idea eventually evolved into LearnServe International, where he partnered with Hugh Riddleberger, the founder of LearnServe, to create programs that empower students to become effective social entrepreneurs.

Scott spoke about the many challenges he had to deal with as a fundraiser and coordinator with his partners, volunteers, parents, and employees. However, his motivation for social entrepreneurship, which stems from his passion for creating positive change and belief in the power of young people to drive social change and transform lives, has kept him from getting discouraged. He has kept his eyes on his goal of encouraging high school students to launch social enterprises and has been willing to evolve the business model of LearnServe International as necessary. Today, LearnServe International relies on a combination of corporate support and its own revenue streams. Before the COVID-19 pandemic, their funding model included earned revue from program enrollment fees, individual contributions, and grants. However, due to the pandemic and the resulting cancellation of their fundraising gala and programs abroad, they had to rely more on philanthropic support.

As a result, the organization has experienced gradual growth, with a focus on passionate, relationship-oriented work that prioritizes empowering young people to address social issues that they care about and aims to eliminate financial barriers to participation. Scott acknowledged the challenges faced in social entrepreneurship, including strategy development, program delivery, fundraising, and staff management. He emphasized the importance of adaptability and problem-solving skills in addressing these challenges. Though Scott sounded content with incremental growth due to limited financial and human resources, the sacrifices, patience, agility, and creative problem-solving in dealing with the many trials and tribulations that come with being committed to social entrepreneurship came through both subtly and directly in his responses throughout the interview.

Over-reliance of bricolage can also lead to challenges and undesired outcomes. For example, a social entrepreneur highlighted the lack of alignment among the co-founders regarding the business model of their enterprise. While he was willing to do what it takes to raise impact capital, his partner and co-founder preferred to pursue donations and grants to fund the enterprise. He expressed frustration and fatigue at having to burn the candle at both ends, running a full-time paying business while also working on their social venture on a volunteer basis for several years. It was clear that this prolonged bricoleur behavior was causing anxiety for him and creating existential challenges for their enterprise.

Extant literature identifies bricolage as a prevalent behavior among social entrepreneurs. Bacq, Ofstein, Kickul, and Gundry (2015) examined the role of bricolage behavior in social entrepreneurs on a broader scale versus being limited to the challenges of limited financial resources. In fact, bricolage can be used when dealing with other related matters such as financing sources and structures, customers and networks, volunteers and employees, office space and physical assets, etc.

Di Domenico, Tracey, and Haugh's (2010) research on bricolage as a theoretical framework for social entrepreneurship provided three key constructs of bricolage as "making do," refusing to be constrained by limitations, and improvisation. They identified three broad characteristics related to social entrepreneurship: social value creation, stakeholder participation, and persuasion. First, social enterprises are primarily driven by the need to create social value through financing achieved via commercial activity, conflating the need to achieve the social and economic goals of the enterprise. Second, creating social and economic value at scale requires the reliance on stakeholders for funding, operations, and advocacy. Finally, social enterprises usually have limited resources and must rely on the power of persuasion to operate and grow their enterprise.

Perkmann and Spicer (2014) extended the studies on bricolage further and introduced the concept of "organizational bricolage," a process through which a new enterprise is formed by using the lessons learned and the business models of existing enterprises. This ability to improvise enables a social entrepreneur to scale the venture's social impact even with minimal resources. Bricoleurs often refuse to accept the lack of resources as a limitation. Instead, they seize opportunities to combine resources, both inside and outside of the enterprise.

Witell et al. (2017) described four capabilities of a bricoleur: the ability to deal with resource constraints; "making do" with existing resources; combining and reallocating resources as needed through improvisation; and networking and fundraising with external partners and stakeholders. Janssen, Fayolle, and Wuilaume (2018) studied the bricolage construct in terms of effectuation and improvisation. Effectuation is an interactive and dynamic process that utilizes logic and entrepreneurial expertise to create new models for solving social issues. It enables the social entrepreneur to choose between possible options that can be created with the existing resources. Improvisation is a process that combines creativity, intuition, and bricolage resulting in the development and execution of the chosen alternative. Similarly, Azmat, Ferdous, and Couchman (2015) provided three constructs of bricolage: making do, refusing to be constrained by limitations, and improvising. The common elements in all these studies and definitions of bricolage point to the ability of a social entrepreneur to create social value through collective entrepreneurship, driven by the mobilization of stakeholders through strong marketing, communication, persuasion, and negotiation skills.

While my informants validated these elements of bricolage behavior, they also expanded on the previous findings to include the factors that generate such behaviors in social entrepreneurs. Previous research addressed the use of bricolage behaviors, whereas my research revealed the factors that lead social entrepreneurs to acquire the attributes of being a bricoleur. These factors include their individual experiences in childhood and their ongoing experimentation and learning from failure. Hence, it is largely a self-taught skill and attribute that social entrepreneurs must embrace to survive and thrive in social entrepreneurship.

CHAPTER 18:

PROSELYTIZER – BRILLIANT PROMOTER

The art of selling is also an extremely important attribute for social entrepreneurs. My informants recounted numerous experiences of their constant need to market and sell their ideas and mission to other players, with the goal of convincing them to become involved and engaged with the enterprise as funders, partners, board members, advisors, or volunteers. Scott Beale, Founder, Board Member, and former CEO of Atlas Corps relayed his experiences with his vast network, from whom he gained his strength. Throughout his journey, which included many years of public service in the government and then launching his social enterprise, he spoke of the many hardships of social entrepreneurship, without much financial reward. He described his dissatisfaction with the actual results, not because they weren't achieving incremental successes, but because of his constant belief that he could have done more. Like many other social entrepreneurs, Scott expressed genuine appreciation for his family, friends, network, and community, and said that their moral and financial support have been critical in order to deal with the many ongoing challenges of launching and running his social enterprise. He emphasized the importance of constantly selling and messaging the mission and values of the enterprise externally and the importance of having a group of people in your corner who will help you get through the rough patches.

Another social entrepreneur provided a good understanding of the social entrepreneurship landscape in Israel and shared his deep sense of satisfaction in doing something to improve society. He also expressed frustration at the lack of support from investors and wealthy individuals but resolved to continue to help social entrepreneurs overcome these and other challenges. His passion for the social sector was evident when he spoke of being addicted to social change, and falling in love with his enterprise to the point of merging his personal identity with the organization. This deep association can also lead to social entrepreneurs' downfall if they are unable to step back or step away even for the good of the organization. He added that the constant selling and seeking financial and other resources that are so essential for the enterprise can also be extremely exhausting for social entrepreneurs and can make them opinionated, impatient, and short-tempered. However, they must always keep an open mind regarding the opinions of others and never stop trying to persuade and convince them to become allies and supporters of the social cause.

Another informant showed genuine emotion in describing how she fell in love with community-based philanthropy in her early years. She went on to study law and worked as an attorney for 20 years but described how restless she had felt for several years and how unfulfilled she was with her law practice. Once she felt that her family's financial security had been achieved, she decided to leave her law practice to become a social entrepreneur. She spoke with great conviction about her experience with elementary school children and was quite troubled by the gender differences in terms of boys' and girls' views about and interest in technology. After a few attempts, she received a grant for $7,000 and was able to launch her enterprise to expose elementary school girls to technology in a fun and non-threatening environment. Several years later, she left her start-up to become the CEO of a community foundation. Though she was initially unhappy and anxious about doing so, she felt that it would give her the opportunity to engage with the whole community and make an even greater impact. The energy she derives from the community could be heard in her responses. However, her enthusiasm was curbed by her fear of being fired by the board because she was moving too fast. She feared that if they did not support a significant change to the foundation's strategy, the foundation would become obsolete. She was frustrated that administrative work and board relations left no time for mission-related work. She was also exhausted by the constant challenges she had to deal with, including the ongoing education, selling, and persuading of her employees, board, and the community players. I could sense the angst and worry in her voice as she prepared to step down and hand over the reins to a new CEO. She recognized the need to separate her personal ego from creating a model for lasting change, even if that meant turning that model over to someone else and trusting them to keep it moving forward.

Another social entrepreneur spoke fondly of his friendships in high school and initially starting several local ventures in his neighborhood. The sense of camaraderie and joy came through in his responses, which made these ventures fun, adventurous, and helpful to the community. I could tell that he really enjoyed this phase of his life. His tone became more serious and somber in describing how deeply affected he was by the misery that the 2008 financial crisis caused in society. In response, he started a non-profit venture. However, he was very frustrated by the constant need to seek government grants and donations. This constant need to beg for money drove him to leave the non-profit and enter the world of social entrepreneurship. Unfortunately, he discovered that he now had to beg for capital from investors, although this will make it possible for him to grow the organization and its programs to provide greater value to the world.

These provide only a few examples of social entrepreneurs being proselytizers. Previous research on commercial entrepreneurs suggests that their social skills – meaning the competencies that help them communicate effectively, interact, and develop relationships with others – may play a role in their success (Baron & Markman, 2000). Their social capital, built on their reputation, market credibility, previous experience, and personal relationships, can help social entrepreneurs access venture capitalists, potential partners, and stakeholders. These social skills, including social perception, impression management, persuasion, social influence, and social adaptability are very beneficial in managing the tensions and trade-offs that social entrepreneurs face.

Previous research has established these skills in terms of a social entrepreneur's human capital and social capital, broadly defined as the supportive resources provided by their social networks. These skills enable a social entrepreneur to manage and resolve various tensions and trade-offs that ultimately determine the success of the enterprise. Previous research has identified three dimensions of social capital: structural, relational, and cognitive (Nahapiet & Ghoshal, 1998). Whether social capital is merely embedded in relationships or reflective of the norms and values associated with such relationships, it is widely accepted that social capital enables the creation of social value. Social and human capital are necessary ingredients for social entrepreneurs to create alignment, goodwill, trust, and credibility with their stakeholders. These traits, combined with selling, convincing, persuading, and negotiating skills make a social entrepreneur operate as a proselytizer.

My informants revealed that as proselytizers, social entrepreneurs are the ultimate salespeople. They are always selling their ideas, with the goal of enlisting partners and stakeholders to join and support their social movement.

CHAPTER 19:
SEDULOUS –
RELENTLESSLY RESILIENT

Social entrepreneurs share other characteristics, such as resilience, dedication, diligence, and unwillingness to give up. Collectively, I group these attributes as sedulousness. These attributes were evident in all the social entrepreneurs that I spoke with. Since 2018, Nancy Welsh has been the Co-Founder, Chief Marketing Officer, and Chief Operating Officer of iBUILD Global, Inc., a for-profit, for-good software development company that has pioneered financially inclusive technology for the under-served, and has also facilitated growth of the housing market with transparency and accountability while providing access to jobs in the construction sector. Through the projects undertaken by this organization, Nancy builds resilient infrastructure, promotes inclusive and sustainable industrialization, and fosters innovation.

Nancy's interest in social entrepreneurship started at a very young age, when she was only eight years old. She shared her experiences with helping a few troubled classmates in elementary school, resulting in her leading an after-school program to help other children in need throughout the school. Nancy defined these as life-changing moments for her that, coupled with her Christian faith and Sunday school classes, further reinforced her values and ignited her desire to help others.

Nancy has started numerous social ventures, often driven by identifying specific problems and devising workable solutions. For example, she started an NGO focused on green communities and even obtained a patent for her solution to rescue houses from demolition, relocate them, and create green affordable housing communities within city limits. Nancy believes that social entrepreneurship is a part of her character and DNA and spoke fondly of her parents, faith, and being taught to live by the golden rule. However, her idealism was tempered by the harsh reality of needing steady income to support her growing family. She shared that once she realized how difficult it was to "do good" in the world, requiring far more sacrifices and stamina that she would have ever realized, she had to drill down on her idea, keep building and innovating, and commit to perseverance. This led to her devising new methods of construction and new partnerships for a reduced cost workforce to further drive sustainability of the model without sacrificing affordability for the beneficiaries. She spoke of the high degree of dedication and discipline required to live within limited means both on a personal level as well as within the social enterprise. This was a life lesson that she would take with her throughout her social entrepreneurship journey. Though she spoke of her privilege of having a family to help fund her first social venture, she had to face numerous challenges that led to the failure of four of her eight social ventures, but she refused to give up. The entrepreneurial mindset that "failure leads to opportunity" fuels her ongoing efforts towards retooling new, more sustainable pathways to solve existing problems with greater impact and resiliency.

Like all other social entrepreneurs who I spoke with, Nancy also stressed the many difficulties in launching and operating a social venture, including the roadblocks she encountered due to her gender and the significant effort it took to overcome social and cultural barriers, despite delivering exceptional benefits and opportunities for otherwise unmet needs. She emphasized the importance of working from the bottom up, building relationships, and amassing intimate knowledge of the problems you are trying to solve. This approach has provided greater credibility to her ideas and has afforded her the confidence and perseverance to position the idea in the market, connect multi-lateral partners, generate revenue, and engage networks to ultimately solve societal problems. She encourages young people to start early on their social entrepreneur journey, seek affirmation for their ideas, learn from failures, and surround themselves with a supportive team.

Tessie San Martin (former President and CEO of Plan International USA and the current CEO of FHI360) spoke of her passion for international development work since she was a teenager. Early in her career, she followed a more traditional path of consulting for many years before entering the social sector on a full-time basis. Having worked in the for-profit sector first, she expressed her disappointment in the non-profit model, which she felt was not held to the same rigor and standards. Given their focus on social missions, she claimed that non-profits, if not managed appropriately, can function as mediocre organizations with little accountability for achieving results. She is working hard to change that model and culture in her organization by creating a different model that is centered on impact capital for self-sufficiency. She had met with some resistance both internally and externally but was determined to keep forging ahead.

Another social entrepreneur who has dedicated his entire life to social service spoke of his grandiose plans to change the world and then getting mired in the realities of raising capital, energizing volunteers, stakeholders, and community leaders, and building relationships with the board. He expressed sadness at having to lay off staff during the economic downturn and at one point, feared his board was going to fire him for moving too quickly. Despite these hurdles, when he received job offers from the for-profit sector with a much higher salary, his sense of duty and keen desire to never give up led him to choose to remain in the social sector. He expressed sadness at leaving the enterprise due to his stage of life and family obligations but noted that new leadership is necessary to keep the organization from stagnating.

Indira Kumar (Co-Founder of India International School and Founder of the Global Economic Foundation) spoke about her village in South America where she grew up and her desire to help and give back to improve the living conditions and lives of children in her village. She spoke of enlisting volunteers and partners – both on the ground in her village as well as here in the United States to develop programs to help the village. She also spoke of her strong sense of responsibility and duty to serve others, being the oldest of eight siblings in her family. She spoke about her interest in running her own business from a young age and did that first, before extending her entrepreneurial spirit to the social sector. I sensed exhaustion in her voice when she spoke of the many challenges she has faced in staying afloat and how difficult this journey has been for her. She recounted with disappointment about her social enterprise nearly having to shut down during COVID-19, but with great personal perseverance and the support of volunteers and the community, it managed to stay afloat. In closing, she expressed great disappointment and surprise that others, who have achieved great successes and riches in life, do not do more for their community and society at large. However, she is committed to continuing the fight and refuses to give up.

As evidenced by the examples provided here, sedulousness is an inherent attribute and one that is somewhat unique to social entrepreneurs. Previous studies on the personal dispositions, intentions, and motivations of social entrepreneurs have emphasized the element of empathy (Lambrechts, Caniels, Molderez, Venn, & Oorbeek, 2020). It is widely accepted that moral empathy is an important trait for social entrepreneurs. Such empathy may develop from a personal experience or a critical event and may drive the motivation to pursue social entrepreneurship. However, what keeps social entrepreneurs motivated and leads to their successful ventures is their sedulousness. This attribute enables social entrepreneurs to subsist, survive, and thrive in the face of numerous challenges and tensions and plays a key role in helping them manage the dual objectives of creating social and economic value. Their sedulousness helps them withstand the many struggles they encounter throughout the life cycle of their social entrepreneurship, regardless of whether they are fully or partially funded, self-sufficient, or barefoot entrepreneurs (Imas, Wilson, & Weston, 2012) who operate in marginal contexts and often live poverty. As I was able to gather from my interviews, social entrepreneurship does not always lead to success stories. Indeed, the perpetual trials and tribulations that social entrepreneurs face reflect the constant struggles, tensions, and indebtedness that often lead to failure. However, it is their sedulousness that results in them choosing to learn from their failures, adapting or pivoting as needed, and simply refusing to give up.

CHAPTER 20:

OPPORTUNIST –
VIGOROUSLY ENTERPRISING

Several of my informants shared experiences that highlighted their opportunistic attribute. Robert Egger (Founder of DC Central Kitchen and LA Kitchen) spoke about his early influences – Cesar Chavez, Martin Luther King, Jr., Robert Kennedy – and having had a vision at age 10 of himself becoming a liberator of sorts. He reminisced about watching the movie "Casablanca" and the impact it had on his own thinking regarding using purposeful entertainment as an outlet for people during difficult times. He made no excuses about not having a college degree but that he always knew he was meant to help society. He was appreciative for being born with a white man's privilege that gave him the confidence to dream, to take risks, and to be heard. He was able to leverage his gender and race to help in connecting with partners and organizations to help launch and operate his social enterprise. He spoke of making a cold call to the United States President's Inauguration organizers to ask them to donate leftover food to his organization and was surprised at how easily they agreed to do it. He spoke about despising charities that rely on donations and has a philosophy to do the opposite of what charities do, by seizing opportunities with the government, organizations, community leaders, and partners to create a self-sustaining business model for his social enterprise. He was also quite transparent about sharing his own strengths of creating and selling, and his weaknesses when it came to running companies. He expressed frustration about his battles with bureaucracy in the county government that contributed to his failed venture in California. Through his many struggles and successes, he regarded his proudest and biggest accomplishment as being able to make payroll for 30 years and solving multiple problems for his community, which included creating jobs, helping the elderly, and feeding the hungry. In his retirement, he is proud to be helping young entrepreneurs by being on the speakers' circuit, writing books, and giving back in other ways.

Similarly, Carrie Rich (Co-Founder and CEO of The Global Good Fund) recounted how she felt privileged throughout her life, which helped her in the co-launch and running of her social enterprise. Her privileges included growing up in a stable and secure environment, her initiative in designing her own major in college, obtaining her first job through her network, and then befriending a CEO who became her mentor, gave her opportunities to grow and learn, and later co-founded the social enterprise with her. She spoke of her challenges as a young, female CEO who seized the opportunity to work closely with a CEO and board chair, and learned to fight for a seat at the table where she could have a voice and be heard.

Nick Cuttriss (Co-Founder and Board Chairman of AYUDA) teamed up with his friend Jesse Fuchs-Simon when they were high school teenagers at Georgetown Day School to do something to help children around the world suffering with diabetes. He said he was happy and fortunate to have grown up in a financially secure environment, so he never had to worry about making ends meet. He felt privileged to have good friends and a strong family network. In fact, during the start-up phase, he called on his parents' network to support his diabetes awareness campaign and educational venture in other parts of the world.

Gretchen Zucker (Founder of Fieldstone Trust LLC) spoke about her early ventures and was beaming with pride that Ashoka was featured in MIT's recruiting materials. She expressed deep gratitude to Ashoka for introducing her to social entrepreneurship. She was passionate about living a purposeful life and determined that nothing would prevent her from doing so. She expressed her fear of failure and being scared about taking significant risks in her latest venture. However, she spoke of making tough decisions, leveraging opportunities through relationships, and being selective about which investors and real estate partners to work with. For example, she had to fire a donor due to issues with mission and values alignment. She too has been fortunate to have had personal financial stability throughout her life and was thankful to have her family, friends, and a network to rely on to support her and her ventures.

Previous studies on entrepreneurs have identified several categories of entrepreneurs: habitual entrepreneurs, portfolio entrepreneurs, and serial entrepreneurs (Lerch, Kirschenhofer, & Dowling, 2016). Habitual entrepreneurs are defined as entrepreneurs who have launched one or more businesses prior to the launch of the current new business and typically create and implement business ideas in partnership with others. Portfolio entrepreneurs are defined as entrepreneurs who are engaged in several businesses simultaneously. Serial entrepreneurs are defined as entrepreneurs who typically start up a new enterprise from their existing one.

It is well-established that the most common ingredient and the greatest requirement for all entrepreneurs is the need for financial capital. This need is most critical for nascent social entrepreneurs, not only during the launch phase when capital constraints are the greatest, but also throughout their business life cycle to enable sustainable operations and provide a reserve or buffer in case of emergencies and unforeseen circumstances. Due to the lack of an industry structure for social capital investment and fundraising, social entrepreneurs often lack access to financing through formal investors and instead must rely on personal networks of family and friends to finance their social enterprises. As a result, social entrepreneurs must be opportunistic in leveraging their networks to seek funding and support for their social enterprise.

Many social entrepreneurs spoke of taking advantage of and leveraging their privilege with respect to their race, gender, secure and stable environment, family wealth, and wealthy networks. Although this attribute may appear at odds with their overall altruism, it is a necessary trait that social entrepreneurs must have to achieve their social and financial goals.

CHAPTER 21:
CONSCIOUS DREAMER – RIGHTEOUS ENTREPRENEUR

The phrase "conscious dreamer," a term used by Dhananjaya Kumar (Co-Founder of India International School and RENEW), describes another key social entrepreneurial attribute. It describes the ability of a social entrepreneur to develop a vision that is aspirational and transformational, while also establishing realistic and practical milestones and measures of success regarding the achievement of that vision. Roshan Paul (Co-Founder and Former CEO of The Amani Institute) shared his genuine gratitude to his parents, who encouraged him to do what makes him happy instead of following the traditional path that is often expected in Asian households. He spoke with great excitement and energy about the need for constant prototyping and having a strong network to draw upon for resources and ideas. His determination, persistence, and stubbornness came across clearly when he spoke of risk-taking, making personal sacrifices, and refusing to give up in the face of adversity. He sounded like an idealist and a dreamer when he spoke about having inspired people to work for him for free until he could pay them, and for hiring people with aligned values versus having the technical skillsets required for the job. He also sounded a bit exhausted and had mixed feelings when he spoke of having turned over his enterprise to a new CEO recently after 10 years. His parting words resonated with me. He said a social entrepreneur's job is never done – the more we serve, the more we see that there is so much more left to be done.

Another social entrepreneur spoke of having grown up with a severe learning disability and family values that encouraged social change rather than making money. She spoke of her humble beginnings but not in a critical or regretful way. Her responses and emotions were sincere as she spoke of feeling rich inside by helping others and achieving social outcomes. Throughout her life, she has taken risks, gone to new and unfamiliar regions of the world, and engaged with the communities in those places to improve their conditions. She became quite emotional at one point speaking of her meager living arrangements over several years due to lack of funds, but she seemed happy and at peace with her choices. She appeared genuinely surprised, realizing in hindsight, that she has been able to accomplish so much with so little over her lifetime. She spoke of being a feminist since she was a child and that it was important for her to pursue women's issues and to empower women. She recalled having worked in Morocco in a small village and having two women start an organization to support other women. She was living on less than $300 a month, but it was sufficient, though it barely covered her expenses.

Another informant appeared to be a very down-to-earth and practical individual who has served her community and helped several other communities around the world throughout her life. Her responses showed an ingrained desire to help others – on the ground and one person at a time. She spoke of having a revelation at age 25 that social entrepreneurship could in fact be a profession and a way of life. She noted with frustration the stigma attached to charitable organizations as always begging for money. At one point, she left the social sector to work for a large, well-paying for-profit organization to earn a better living but was dissatisfied and unfulfilled. Therefore, she returned to a lower paying job in a social enterprise. She also expressed disappointment and frustration with the bureaucratic legal processes involved in launching a social enterprise and the difficulty that she faced repeatedly with raising capital. She emphasized the need for a social entrepreneur to have business skills and to work in partnership with other players in launching an enterprise. Her skepticism came through when sharing her experiences with social entrepreneurs and enterprises that begin with a lofty social mission but quickly turn their focus to revenue growth and diversification. Her belief is that to help society at scale, a social enterprise must have a successful business model, noting that having a social mission is simply not enough. She was inspired to continually fight to change the system, as she saw that social entrepreneurship became a part of her character and that she wants to continue to help people, give back, design and devise solutions that provide a recurring benefit to the underserved.

Burck Smith (Founder and Former CEO of StraighterLine) entered the social entrepreneurship field nearly 25 years ago expecting that social entrepreneurship might not be that different from traditional entrepreneurship. The ongoing challenges of raising capital, dealing with venture capital firms, and operating an enterprise confirmed that. He sounded resolved in sharing his experiences and his realization that social entrepreneurship might be a misnomer, a feel-good label for the entrepreneur and his or her investors. He began to feel that, ultimately, a social enterprise is just looking to survive, like other enterprises. Being a true entrepreneur, he negotiated an exit with his venture capitalists in 2009 and was able to spin-off another social venture. He sounded very pragmatic when he spoke of selling his second venture to a private equity firm that, like almost all investors (social and otherwise), placed a higher priority on financial returns over social returns. He spoke with great passion about being motivated by his venture's social mission and how that helped him deal with life and death moments by just refusing to give up. He also expressed sorrow and disappointment at having to lay off staff when times were difficult.

However, at one point, he became quite reflective and began to question the distinction between social entrepreneurship and traditional entrepreneurship. For instance, his company's mission – to lower the cost of general education college courses – would help students but harm some colleges. In this and other similar cases, one person's or entity's social good may become another's social harm. He also spoke of how fortunate he had been, including having had the privilege of an elite education, a stable family, and a well-connected social network, coupled with luck and good timing. Overall, his thinking about social entrepreneurship seems to have evolved, in that while the enterprise's mission may be a good one, it is the financial performance that keeps the investors happy and the enterprise viable.

The term "conscious dreaming" is often used in the study of dreams with regard to people's ability to connect with their dreams in a conscious state. However, my use of the term refers to the ability of social entrepreneurs to create a bold, aspirational, transformational vision, with their ability to tackle realistic and practical short-term goals and milestones with great empathy and compassion.

Pittz, Madden, and Mayo (2017) highlighted compassion - defined as a feeling or desire to ease the pain and suffering of others - as a key motivator that enables social entrepreneurs to develop big dreams to bring about systemic change. The ability of social entrepreneurs to dream big is also driven by their optimism. In fact, previous research shows that entrepreneurs possess an elevated sense of dispositional optimism, defined as the propensity to expect positive outcomes even in the face of adversity or when such positive expectations may not be rational and may appear to be unattainable. This sense of optimism drives social entrepreneurs to pursue their lofty vision and dreams despite the challenges they face.

In this regard, my informants did show some evidence of social entrepreneurs viewing the world through idealistic and somewhat rose-colored glasses. They believed that regardless of the barriers, in the end, everything would eventually work out for the best. This optimism reflected their contentment with doing the right thing and hoping for a favorable result without seeking a guaranteed outcome. This sense of duty drives social entrepreneurs to live through self-empowerment.

Haugh and Talwar (2014) defined empowerment as resulting in the removal of barriers in an individual's ability or capacity to make choices and decisions, giving the individual the ability to make decisions from a position of authority and strength. They described five types of empowerment: economic empowerment (accessibility to income); social empowerment (position and status in the community); political empowerment (engagement in the public sector), cultural empowerment (a feeling of belonging in society), and personal empowerment (having the confidence to act and make choices).

All my informants exhibited a strong sense of personal empowerment to develop and pursue their dreams for a better society but in a manner that acknowledged the harsh realities and daunting challenges of the social entrepreneurial environment.

CHAPTER 22:

SUMMARY

Our planet is facing numerous grand challenges in many key areas that impact the existence and sustainability of humanity. Social entrepreneurs play a major role in addressing these challenges. In this book, I have provided insights into the many tensions and trade-offs that social entrepreneurs must balance on a daily basis, as well as the coping mechanisms they must deploy to manage, mitigate, overcome, or accept the many challenges they face in the launch and operation of a social enterprise. I believe that a study of the unique attributes of social entrepreneurs can provide a deeper understanding of their intentions and motivations and insights into their passion and sense of moral obligation not only to solve a specific social problem but also to create a framework for lasting change on a global scale.

The Life Cycle of a Social Entrepreneur

Contrary to previous research that has largely defined the life cycle of an enterprise in the context of an entrepreneurial ecosystem or that of an organization, my study provides unique insights into the life cycle of a social entrepreneur. My results identified four stages in the life cycle of a social entrepreneur: entering, launching, operating, and exiting. These insights contrast with previous studies that define a traditional organization's life cycle in terms of birth, growth, maturity, decline, or re-emergence and preparedness, embarkation, exploration, exploitation, and transformation. Further, the life cycle of a social entrepreneur is inseparable from the enterprise. Social entrepreneurs do not view their enterprise as a business but rather as a vehicle that extends their passion and social mission. Since social entrepreneurs do not measure success in monetary terms and are driven by passion over profit, their personal journey, as lived through their enterprise, continues to evolve and transform, as does their social mission and goal.

Balancing Tensions

Tensions and conflicts are inherent in all businesses. However, they are more prevalent and complex in social entrepreneurship. Previous scholars have studied such tensions in social entrepreneurship, but these studies have primarily focused on the inherent conflict between pursuing a social mission and financial goals, resulting in social mission design tensions.

To expand on previous research, I provide a more extensive examination of the various tensions, contradictions, and trade-offs that social entrepreneurs must balance throughout their organization's life cycle. These tensions are existential, moral, inertial, structural, relational, and aptitudinal. Consistent with previous research, existential tension is driven by factors such as the goal of pursuing a social mission and economic goals. However, it also includes the tension between personal financial security and institutional survival. In contrast with previous studies, moral tension includes the balancing of the social entrepreneur's deep sense of moral obligation with increasing levels of cynicism. Inertial tension arises from internal and external forces. Structural tension emanates from the contradiction between flexibility and completeness. Relational tension results from the lack of alignment with stakeholders that becomes a double-edged sword. Finally, aptitudinal tension arises from the skill sets, competencies, and interests of the social entrepreneur. ˙

Subsisting Responses

There is limited research on how social entrepreneurs deal with the myriad of challenges they face throughout their entrepreneurial journey. Although previous studies on topics and theories such as social and entrepreneurial bricolage, social marketing, social capital, stakeholder theory, and the theory of effectual reasoning have researched specific topics in various contexts, there is no previous research on the totality of the coping mechanisms and responses that social entrepreneurs need to deal with their tensions and trade-offs.

Through my interviews, data collection, and analysis, I identified six such subsisting responses: evangelizing, improvising, rallying, persisting, leveraging, and adapting. While a few of these subsisting responses, such as improvising and rallying, are consistent with and expand on previous and related research, others such as evangelizing, persisting, leveraging, and adapting have not been examined previously. It is noteworthy that these subsisting responses are informed and enabled by the imprinting frames and facilitated by the social entrepreneur's unique attributes.

While social entrepreneurs use various coping mechanisms to manage, mitigate, or overcome the tensions they face, I believe that these tensions are typical characteristics of the social sector. Therefore, social entrepreneurs often accept, live with, and work around these tensions and contradictions rather than exert energy and resources to resolve them.

Social Entrepreneurial Attributes

There is an abundance of previous literature on the personality traits of leaders and entrepreneurs. Previous scholars have also researched the personality traits of social entrepreneurs, but only generally and as compared with the traits of traditional entrepreneurs. I have expanded on previous studies to include other attributes that are unique to social entrepreneurs: crusader, bricoleur, proselytizer, sedulous, opportunist, and conscious dreamer. In doing so, I provide a comprehensive and unique set of attributes that define and differentiate social entrepreneurs from traditional entrepreneurs. These service-oriented attributes also expand the definition of metapreneur as applied to the social sector in defining the unique traits that establish social entrepreneurs as a different breed of actors on the social stage.

Grounded Theory

Having reviewed the balancing tensions, subsisting responses, and social entrepreneurial attributes, it is helpful to examine the inter-theme relationships among the three components. As Figure 8 illustrates, the balancing tensions require subsisting responses that are necessary to tackle the various tensions and trade-offs faced by social entrepreneurs. The subsisting responses demand the social entrepreneurial traits that, in essence, promote and are essential to creating the subsisting responses. The subsisting responses allow social entrepreneurs to cope with the various tensions they encounter throughout the lifecycle of their enterprise.

Figure 8. **Grounded Theory**

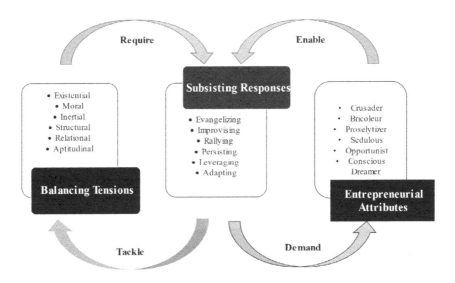

Furthermore, there is a direct correlation between social entrepreneurs' attributes and their subsisting responses. Thus, the coping mechanism of evangelizing is the result of the attribute of being a crusader. Improvising arises from the attribute of being a bricoleur. Rallying is driven by the trait of being a proselytizer. Persistence results from sedulousness. Leveraging is an outgrowth of being an opportunist. Adaptation emanates from a social entrepreneur being a conscious dreamer, having the ability to dream big but having to remain flexible, adaptive, and realistic.

Recommendations

The focus of social entrepreneurship is to develop lasting and enduring solutions to address social problems to change society and the world for the better. Social entrepreneurial and non-profit organizations play an important role in society as they help constituents who are not being adequately served by the government, corporations, and capital markets.

In fact, such market and state failures provide the impetus for the establishment of social enterprises. Having examined the multiple tensions and trade-offs they face and how they manage these tensions, I have identified several factors that would give a much-needed boost to the social entrepreneurial sector and enhance the success of social entrepreneurs.

First, I believe that the infusion of social awareness and a sense of responsibility in early education can play a significant role in incubating social entrepreneurs in their adolescence and adulthood. Although none of my informants was exposed to such education in their early years, all spoke of the strong influence that social entrepreneurship education in higher education and in the workplace had on forming and solidifying their desire to pursue social entrepreneurship. Introducing the concepts of social responsibility, community engagement, and active civic citizenship and responsibility to children in early education can help develop and forge a stronger awareness of their role in society. Consequently, it can promote a stronger sense of collaboration, teamwork, empathy, negotiation, and problem-solving through observation, experience, self-reflection, and volunteerism. Such education can motivate children and adolescents to pursue social entrepreneurship as a career in adulthood. I hope that my research will encourage educators to introduce such programs in early education that will plant the seeds for the future betterment of society.

Second, all social entrepreneurs that I interviewed demonstrated the power of co-creation and collective entrepreneurship with partners and stakeholders within their sectors and local communities. The social impact of such collaboration and co-creation would be exponential if applied across sectors and on a global scale. The network effect of such collaborations, knowledge sharing, and collective problem-solving would create a durable and sustainable framework for social change. Organizations such as Ashoka have created a theory of social change in encouraging and supporting everyone to become a changemaker. However, greater cross-sector and cross-county collaboration is needed to make social ventures scalable through local and global support and to create an operating model for social entrepreneurship.

Third, social entrepreneurs are routinely challenged to provide quantifiable success measures for their social enterprises. While measures of success are fairly standardized in the financial industry, there is a lack of unified industry standards for measuring the value and impact of a social enterprise. In social entrepreneurship, the creation of social value is often an elusive concept. It encompasses a broad array of measures, including the quality and delivery of its programs and projects; the enterprise's ability to raise impact capital; and its ability to sustain its business model with limited resources. While social innovations and disruptions solve societal problems and create social value, there are no standards or tools available to measure such social returns. Perhaps a cross-industry coalition can be formed to tackle this and other key gaps that plague social entrepreneurship.

Fourth, it is universally acknowledged that the lack of sufficient financial capital is the single largest challenge facing social entrepreneurs. Therefore, we need a change in the model for financing social enterprises. Valuing an enterprise's total revenue – commercial and charitable – to access investment capital from traditional sources but with reasonable expectations about the returns can be a game changer for social enterprises. However, doing so would require the development of an industry standard for measuring social value, as described above. Similarly, we also need more standards and regulations to govern social impact investing, meaning investments designed to have a positive social and/or environmental impact as opposed to producing financial value as measured through traditional metrics such as return on investment. Recent developments in investment banking have led to the development of socially responsible investing that is geared towards encouraging investment in certain sectors and industries focusing on solving social and environmental issues. An outgrowth of this development is environmental, social, and governance (ESG) investing that incorporates investment fundamentals and analysis into the evaluation of impact investing. While this is a relatively new investment vehicle that is continuing to develop and evolve in the market, thus far it has had a minimal impact on enabling social entrepreneurship.

Finally, although the government supports social partnerships though grants and programs, such as development of innovation ventures, innovation investment alliances, global development alliances, and diaspora marketplace programs, the government sector must do more to invest in and support social entrepreneurs. Establishing an agency focused on supporting social entrepreneurship domestically as well as a global alliance to support and fund social entrepreneurs engaged in solving global issues should be considered. The government should also consider funding and supporting the creation of a social entrepreneurship model that integrates collaborative efforts across the public, private, and non-government organizations, such that social entrepreneurship becomes ingrained in all sectors as a necessary component of their organizational mission and vision.

In conclusion, this book highlights the intricate, complex, and evolving landscape of social entrepreneurship, that is fraught with significant challenges. These challenges give rise to numerous tensions and tradeoffs that social entrepreneurs must balance on an ongoing basis. Through my extensive research and experience, I have provided practical insights and strategies to navigate and/or embrace these complexities inherent in the sector, enabling social entrepreneurs to foster positive impact, ultimately contributing to a more sustainable and equitable future for our future generations.

REFERENCES

Ajzen, I. (1991). "The Theory of Planned Behavior," Organizational Behavior and Human Decision Processes 50, 179–211. Alvord, S., Brown, D., and Letts, C. 2002. *Social Entrepreneurship and Social Transformation: An Exploratory Study.* Cambridge, MA.

Austin, J., Stevenson, H., & Wei–Skillern, J. (2006). Social and Commercial Entrepreneurship: Same, Different, or Both? *Entrepreneurship Theory and Practice*, 30(1), 1–22. https://doi.org/10.1111/j.1540-6520.2006.00107.x.

Azmat, F. (2015). Understanding the Dynamics Between Social Entrepreneurship and Inclusive Growth in Subsistence Marketplaces. *Journal of Public Policy & Marketing*, 34(2), 252–271. https://doi.org/10.1509/jppm.14.150

Bacq, O. (2015). Bricolage in Social Entrepreneurship: How Creative Resource Mobilization Fosters Greater Social Impact. *International Journal of Entrepreneurship and Innovation*, 16(4), 283–289. https://doi.org/10.5367/ijei.2015.0198.

Baker, M. (2003). Improvising firms: bricolage, account giving and improvisational competencies in the founding process. *Research Policy*, 32(2), 255–276. https://doi.org/10.1016/s0048-7333(02)00099-9.

Baker, N. (2005). Creating Something from Nothing: Resource Construction through Entrepreneurial Bricolage. *Administrative*

Science Quarterly, 50(3), 329–366. https://doi.org/10.2189/asqu.2005.50.3.329.

Baron, R. A., & Markman, G. D. (2000). Beyond social capital: How social skills can Enhance entrepreneurs' success. *The Academy of Management Executive, 14*(1), 106-116. doi: http://dx.doi.org.ezproxy2.library.drexel.edu/10.5465/ame.2000.2909843.

Batson, C.D., Ahmad, N., Powell, A.A., & Stocks, E.L. (2008). Prosocial motivation. In J.Y. Shah & W.L. Gardner (Eds.), *Handbook of Motivation Science* (pp. 135–149). New York: Guilford Press.

Battilana, D. (2010). Building Sustainable Hybrid Organizations: The Case of Commercial Microfinance Organizations. *Academy of Management Journal*, 53(6), 1419–1440. https://doi.org/10.5465/AMJ.2010.57318391.

Battilana, J. (2006). Agency and Institutions: The Enabling Role of Individuals' Social Position. *Organization,* 13(5), 653–676. https://doi.org/10.1177/1350508406067008.

Benford, R. D,, & Snow, D. A. (2000). Framing processes and social movements: An overview and assessment. *Annual Review of Sociology*, 26, 611-639

Benjamin CG. 2006. *Towards an integrated theory of entrepreneurship*. Swinburne University of Technology, Melbourne. Retrieved from http://hdl.handle.net/1959.3/27946

Blau, P. (1964). *Exchange and power in social life.* J. Wiley.

Boeker, W. (1989). Strategic Change: The Effects of Founding and History. *Academy of Management Journal*, 32(3), 489–515. https://doi.org/10.2307/256432.

Bojica, R. (2018). Bricolage and growth in social entrepreneurship organizations. *Entrepreneurship and Regional Development*, 30(3-4), 362–389. https://doi.org/10.1080/08985626.2017.1413768.

Bornstein, D. (2007). *David Bornstein lecture: social entrepreneurship. Bottom up approach to microfinance.* Prendismo.

Bryant, P. (2014). Imprinting by Design: The Microfoundations of Entrepreneurial Adaptation. *Entrepreneurship Theory and Practice*, 38(5), 1081–1102. https://doi.org/10.1111/j.1540-6520.2012.00529.x.

Burga, R., & Rezania, D. (2016). Stakeholder theory in social entrepreneurship: A descriptive case study. *Journal of Global Entrepreneurship Research*, 6(1), 1-15. doi: http://dx.doi.org.ezproxy2.library.drexel.edu/10.1186/s40497-016-0049-8.

Chan, W., Ou, S., & Reynolds, A. (2014). Adolescent Civic Engagement and Adult Outcomes: An Examination Among Urban Racial Minorities. *Journal of Youth and Adolescence*, 43(11), 1829–1843. https://doi.org/10.1007/s10964-014-0136-5.

Charmaz, K. (2006). *Constructing grounded theory: A practical guide through qualitative analysis.* Sage.

Charmaz, K. (2014). *Constructing grounded theory.* Sage.

Cohen, H., & Katz, H. (2016). Social entrepreneurs narrating their careers: A psychodynamic-existential perspective. *Australian*

Journal of Career Development, 25(2), 78–88. https://doi.org/10.1177/1038416216658046

Coplan, A. (2011). Will the real empathy please stand up? A case for a narrow conceptualization. *South. J. Philos.* 49, 40–65. doi: 10.1111/j.2041-6962.2011.00056.x

Davidsson, P., Baker, T., & Senyard, J. M. (2017). A measure of entrepreneurial bricolage behavior. *International Journal of Entrepreneurial Behaviour & Research, 23*(1), 114-135. doi: http://dx.doi.org.ezproxy2.library.drexel.edu/10.1108/IJEBR-11-2015-0256.

Davis, L. (2019). Collective Social Identity: Synthesizing Identity Theory and Social Identity Theory Using Digital Data. *Social Psychology Quarterly*, 82(3), 254–273. https://doi.org/10.1177/0190272519851025.

Dees, J., Economy, P., & Emerson, J. (2001). *Enterprising nonprofits: a toolkit for social entrepreneurs.* Wiley.

Denis, J., Lamothe, L., & Langley, A. (2001). The Dynamics of Collective Leadership and Strategic Change in Pluralistic Organizations. *The Academy of Management Journal, 44*(4), 809-837. Retrieved from www.jstor.org/stable/3069417.

Desa, G., & Basu, S. (2013). Optimization or Bricolage? Overcoming Resource Constraints in Global Social Entrepreneurship. *Strategic Entrepreneurship Journal*, 7(1), 26–49. https://doi.org/10.1002/sej.1150

Di Domenico, H. (2010). Social Bricolage: Theorizing Social Value Creation in Social Enterprises. *Entrepreneurship*

Theory and Practice, 34(4), 681–703. https://doi.
org/10.1111/j.1540-6520.2010.00370.x

DiMaggio, P. (1988) 'Interest and Agency in Institutional Theory', in
L. Zucker (ed.) *Institutional Patterns and Organizations*, pp. 3–22.
Cambridge, MA: Ballinger.

Ehrhart, N. (2004). Organizational Citizenship Behavior in Work
Groups: A Group Norms Approach. *Journal of Applied Psychology*,
89(6), 960–974. https://doi.org/10.1037/0021-9010.89.6.960.

Elkington, J. (1994). Towards the Sustainable Corporation:
Win-Win-Win Business Strategies for Sustainable Development.
California Management Review, 36(2), 90–100. https://doi.
org/10.2307/41165746.

Erikson, T. (2002). Entrepreneurial capital: The emerging venture's
most important asset and competitive advantage. *Journal of Business
Venturing, 17*(3), 275-290.

Espinoza-Benavides, J., & Díaz, D. (2019). The entrepreneurial profile
after failure. *International Journal of Entrepreneurial Behaviour &
Research, 25*(8), 1634-1651. doi: http://dx.doi.org.ezproxy2.library.
drexel.edu/10.1108/IJEBR-04-2018-0242.

Ferraro, F., Etzion, D., & Gehman, J. (2015). Tackling
Grand Challenges Pragmatically: Robust Action
Revisited. *Organization Studies, 36*(3), 363–390. https://doi.
org/10.1177/0170840614563742.

Freeman, R. (1994). The Politics of Stakeholder Theory: Some Future
Directions. *Business Ethics Quarterly*, 4(4), 409–421. https://doi.
org/10.2307/3857340.

Gardner, H. (2004). *A multiplicity of intelligences: In tribute to professor Luigi Vignolo.* Retrieved February, 11(1976), 2008 Retrieved from http://citeseerx.ist.psu.edu/viewdoc/summary?doi=10.1.1.73.364.

Garud, R., Jain, S., & Tuertscher, P. (2008). Incomplete by Design and Designing for Incompleteness. *Organization Studies*, 29(3), 351–371. https://doi.org/10.1177/0170840607088018.

Goyal, S., Sergi, B. and Jaiswal, M. (2016), Understanding the challenges and strategic actions of social entrepreneurship at base of the pyramid, *Management Decision*, Vol. 54 No. 2, pp. 418-440. https://doi.org/10.1108/MD-11-2014-0662.

Grant, A.M. (2007). Relational job design and the motivation to make a prosocial difference. *Academy of Management Review, 32,* 393–417.

Greenleaf, R. (1977). *Servant Leadership: a journey into the nature of legitimate power and greatness.* Paulist Press.

Harrison, R. T., Mason, C. M., & Girling, P. (2004). Financial bootstrapping and venture development in the software industry. *Entrepreneurship and Regional Development*, 16, 307-333.

Imas, J. M., Wilson, N., & Weston, A. (2012). Barefoot Entrepreneurs. *Organization, 19*(5), 563-585.

Janssen, F. (2018). Researching bricolage in social entrepreneurship. *Entrepreneurship and Regional Development*, 30(3-4), 450–470. https://doi.org/10.1080/08985626.2017.1413769.

Jebarajakirthy, C., & Thaichon, P. (2015). A conceptual framework for understanding and developing entrepreneurial behaviour: implications for social marketers: Entrepreneurial behaviour. *International Journal of Nonprofit and Voluntary Sector Marketing, 20*(4), 299–311. https://doi.org/10.1002/nvsm.1532

Koe Hwee Nga, J., and Shamuganathan, G. (2010). The influence of personality traits and demographic factors on social entrepreneurship start up intentions. *J. Bus. Ethics* 95, 259–282. doi: 10.1007/s10551-009-0358-8

Kor, Y. Y., Mahoney, J. T., & Michael, S. C. (2007). Resources, Capabilities and Entrepreneurial Perception, *Journal of Management Studies*, 44(7), 1187-1212.

Kotler, P., & Levy, S. (1969). Broadening the concept of marketing. *Journal of Marketing, 33*(1), 10-15.

Krueger, N. F., Reilly, M. D., & Carsrud, A. L. (2000). Competing models of entrepreneurial intentions. *Journal of Business Venturing*, 15(5–6), 411–432.

Lechner, C., Dowling, M., & Welpe, I. (2006). Firm networks and firm development: The role of the relational mix. *Journal of Business Venturing, 21*, 514–540.

Lefebvre RC. 2011. An integrative model for social marketing. *Journal of Social Marketing* 1(1): 54–72.

Lessem, R. (1986). Becoming a Metapreneur. *Journal of General Management*, 11(4), 5–21. https://doi.org/10.1177/030630708601100401.

Levi-Strauss, C. (1966). Anthropology: Its Achievements and Future. *Current Anthropology*, 7(2), 124–127. https://doi.org/10.1086/200688.

Liden, R. C., Wayne, S. J., Chenwei Liao, & Meuser, J. D. (2014). Servant Leadership and Serving Culture: Influence on Individual and Unit Performance. *Academy of Management Journal*, 57(5), 1434–1452. https://doi-org.ezproxy2.library.drexel.edu/10.5465/amj.2013.0034.

Liden, W. (2008). Servant leadership: Development of a multidimensional measure and multi-level assessment. *The Leadership Quarterly*, 19(2), 161–177. https://doi.org/10.1016/j.leaqua.2008.01.006.

López-Núñez, M. I., Rubio-Valdehita, S., Aparicio-Garcia, M. E., Diaz-Ramiro, E. M. (2020). Are entrepreneurs born or made? The influence of personality. *Personality and Individual Differences,* 154, 109699–. https://doi.org/10.1016/j.paid.2019.109699.

Mair, J., & Martí, I. (2006). Social entrepreneurship research: A source of explanation, prediction, and delight. *Journal of World Business*, 41(1), 36–44 http://doi.org/10.1016/j.jwb.2005.09.002.

Mair, J., & Noboa, E. (2006). Social entrepreneurship: How intentions to create a social Venture are formed. *In Social entrepreneurship* (pp. 121–135). UK: Palgrave Macmillan.

Miller, D., & Sardais, C. (2015). Bifurcating Time: How Entrepreneurs Reconcile the Paradoxical Demands of the Job. *Entrepreneurship Theory and Practice*, 39(3), 489–512. https://doi.org/10.1111/etap.12049

Miner, A. S., Bassoff, P., & Moorman, C. (2001). Organizational improvisation and learning: A field study. *Administrative Science Quarterly*, 46, 304-337.

Mitzinneck, B. C., & Besharov, M. L. (2019). Managing Value Tensions in Collective Social Entrepreneurship: The Role of Temporal, Structural, and Collaborative Compromise. *Journal of Business Ethics*, 159(2), 381–400. https://doi.org/10.1007/s10551-018-4048-2

Montgomery, A., Dacin, P. and Dacin, M. 2012. Collective Social Entrepreneurship: Collaboratively Shaping Social Good. Springer Science and Business Media Dordrecht. Murphy, C. (2009). A Model of Social Entrepreneurial Discovery. *Journal of Business Ethics*, 87(3), 325–336. https://doi.org/10.1007/s10551-008-9921-y.

Nahapiet, J., & Ghoshal, S. (1998). Social capital, intellectual capital, and the organizational advantage. *Academy of Management Review*, 23:242-266

Nicholls, A. (2009). We do good things, don't we? Blended value accounting in social entrepreneurship. *Accounting, Organizations and Society*, 34, 755-69.

Oana, G. & Shahrazad, H. (2013). Does Civil Society Create Social Entrepreneurs? Analele Universităţii din Oradea. *Ştiinţe Economice*, 22(1), 650–657.

Pache, A., & Chowdhury, I. 2012. Social entrepreneurs as institutionally embedded entrepreneurs: Towards a new model of social entrepreneurship education. *Academy of Management Learning & Education*, 11: 494–510.

Penner, L. A., and Finkelstein, M. A. (1998). Dispositional and structural determinants of volunteerism. *J. Pers. Soc. Psychol.* 74, 525–537. doi: 10.1037/0022-3514.74.2.525

Perkmann, M., & Spicer, A. (2014). How Emerging Organizations Take Form: The Role of Imprinting and Values in Organizational Bricolage. *Organization Science* (Providence, R.I.), 25(6), 1785–1806. https://doi.org/10.1287/orsc.2014.0916

Peterson, M. F. (1995). Leading Cuban-American entrepreneurs: The process of Developing motives, abilities and resources. *Human Relations*, 48, 1193-1216.

Petrovskaya, I. and Mirakyan, A. 2018. A Mission of Service: Social Entrepreneur as a Servant Leader, *International Journal of Entrepreneurial Behavior & Research*.

Pittz, T. G., Madden, L. T., & Mayo, D. (2017). Catalyzing social innovation: leveraging compassion and open strategy in social entrepreneurship. *New England Journal of Entrepreneurship*.

Renko, M. (2013). Early Challenges of Nascent Social Entrepreneurs. *Entrepreneurship Theory and Practice*, 37(5), 1045–1069. https://doi.org/10.1111/j.1540-6520.2012.00522.x.

Salamone, A. (1998). On Developing Comparative Nonprofit-Sector Theory: A Reply to Steinberg and Young, and Ragin. *Voluntas (Manchester, England)*, 9(3), 271–281. https://doi.org/10.1023/A:1022014418732.

Sarasvathy, S. D. (2001). Causation and effectuation: Toward a theoretical shift from economic inevitability to entrepreneurial contingency. *Academy of Management. The Academy of Management Review*, 26(2), 243-263. Retrieved from http://ezproxy2.library.drexel.edu/login?url=https://www-proquest-com.ezproxy2.library.drexel.edu/docview/210984203?accountid=10559.

Sarasvathy, S. D. (2004). Making it happen: Beyond theories of the firm to theories of firm design. Entrepreneurship, *Theory and Practice*, *28*, 519-531.

Sautet, F., (2002). *An entrepreneurial theory of the firm*, London: Routledge.

Savitz, A. (2006). The Triple Bottom Line: How Today's Best-Run Companies Are Achieving Economic, Social and Environmental Success -- and How You Can Too. In *The Triple Bottom Line* (1. Aufl.). Jossey-Bass.

Saxton, J. (1996). Five direct marketing strategies for nonprofit organisations. *International Journal of Nonprofit and Voluntary Sector Marketing*, *1*(4), 299–306. https://doi.org/10.1002/nvsm.6090010402

Schwartz, S. H. (1994). Are there universal aspects in the structure and contents of human values? *J. Soc. Issues* 50, 19–45. doi: 10.1111/j.1540-4560.1994.tb01196.x

Semrau, T., & Hopp, C. (2016). Complementary or compensatory? A contingency perspective on how entrepreneurs' human and social capital interact in shaping start-up progress. *Small Business Economics*, *46*(3), 407-423. Retrieved May 31, 2020, from www.jstor.org/stable/43895692.

Siegner, M., Pinkse, J., & Panwar, R. (2018). Managing tensions in a social enterprise: The complex balancing act to deliver a multi-faceted but coherent social mission. *Journal of Cleaner Production*, *174*, 1314–1324. https://doi.org/10.1016/j.jclepro.2017.11.076.

Smith, L. (2011). Toward a Theory of Paradox: A Dynamic Equilibrium Model of Organizing. *The Academy of Management Review*, 36(2), 381–403. https://doi.org/10.5465/AMR.2011.59330958.

Smith, O. (1983). Organizational citizenship behavior: Its nature and antecedents. *Journal of Applied Psychology*, 68(4), 653–663. https://doi.org/10.1037/0021-9010.68.4.653.

Smith, W. K., & Lewis, M. W. 2011. Toward a theory of paradox: A dynamic equilibrium model of organizing. *Academy of Management Review*, 36: 381-403.

Spear, R. (2006). Social entrepreneurship: a different model? *International Journal of Social Economics*, 33(5/6), 399–410. https://doi.org/10.1108/03068290610660670.

Starr, J. R., & MacMillan, I. C. (1990). Resource cooptation via social contracting: Resource acquisition strategies for new ventures. *Strategic Management Journal, 11*, 79-92.

Stets, B. (2000). Identity Theory and Social Identity Theory. *Social Psychology Quarterly*, 63(3), 224–237. https://doi.org/10.2307/2695870.

Tajfel, H. (1972). Some developments in European social psychology. *European Journal of Social Psychology*, 2(3), 307–321. https://doi.org/10.1002/ejsp.2420020307.

Thompson, E. R. (2009) Individual entrepreneurial intent: construct clarification and development of an internationally reliable metric, *Entrepreneurship Theory and Practice, 33*, 669–94.

Thompson, P., Jones-Evans, D., & Kwong, C. (2010). Education and entrepreneurial activity: A comparison of white and South Asian men. *International Small Business Journal*, 28(2), 147–162. https://doi.org/10.1177/0266242609355858.

Thompson, P., & Kwong, C. (2016). Compulsory school-based enterprise education as a gateway to an entrepreneurial career. *International Small Business Journal*, 34(6), 838–869. https://doi.org/10.1177/0266242615592186.

Tiwari, P., Bhat, A., & Tikoria, J. (2017). An empirical analysis of the factors affecting social entrepreneurial intentions. *Journal of Global Entrepreneurship Research*, 7(1), 1–25. https://doi.org/10.1186/s40497-017-0067-1.

van Dierendonck, D. (2011). Servant Leadership: A Review and Synthesis. *Journal of Management*, 37(4), 1228–1261. https://doi.org/10.1177/0149206310380462.

Wernick, L. J. (2012). Leveraging privilege: Organizing young people with wealth to support social justice. *Social Service Review*, 86(2), 323-345.

Wu, S., Matthews, G., & Dagher, G. (2007). Need for achievement, business goals, and entrepreneurial persistence. *Management Research News*, 30(12), 928-941.

Yitshaki, R., & Kropp, F. (2016). Motivations and Opportunity Recognition of Social Entrepreneurs. *Journal of Small Business Management*, 54(2), 546–565. https://doi.org/10.1111/jsbm.12157

Yusuf, S. (2015). Effectual Processes in Nonprofit Start-Ups and Social Entrepreneurship: An Illustrated Discussion of a Novel Decision-Making Approach. *American Review of Public Administration*, 45(4), 417–435. https://doi. org/10.1177/0275074013509685.

Zahra, S. A., Gedajlovic, E., Neubaum, D. O., & Shulman, J. M. (2009). A typology of social entrepreneurs: Motives, search processes and ethical challenges. *Journal of Business Venturing*, 24(5), 519–532.

Zahra, S. A. & Wright, M. (2016). Understanding the Social Role of Entrepreneurship. *Journal of Management Studies*, 53(4), 610–629. https://doi.org/10.1111/jom.

Zhu, R., Rooney, D., & Phillips, N. (2016). Practice-Based Wisdom Theory for Integrating Institutional Logics: A New Model for Social Entrepreneurship Learning and Education. *Academy of Management Learning & Education*, 15(3), 607–625. https://doi. org/10.5465/amle.2013.0263

ABOUT THE AUTHOR

Dr. Usha Chaudhary is a distinguished leader renowned for her transformative impact on organizations across various sectors. As the Chief Operating Officer of The Student Conversation Association, she continues to drive business growth, fiscal discipline, and operational excellence. With a rich executive background in strategy, finance, operations, technology, human resources, and risk management, she has held pivotal roles in globally recognized entities such as Internews, The MITRE Corporation, Kettler, The Pew Charitable Trusts, The Washington Post, United Way of America, and Freddie Mac.

Dr. Chaudhary's commitment extends beyond the corporate realm, as she actively contributes to non-profit and trade associations holding key positions on boards and committees. A fervent advocate for education, she supports charitable organizations focused on enriching youth through structured programs.

Recognized for her outstanding contributions, Dr. Chaudhary has received numerous awards, including Analytics Insight's "Top 10 Most Influential Women in Technology" in 2020, Washingtonian's "Most Powerful Women in Washington" in 2017; Bisnow's "Women of Influence in Commercial Real Estate" in 2017; Washington Business Journal's "Women Who Mean Business" in 2016; and Washington's "Non-Profit CFO of the Year Award for Innovation" in 2007.